AUTH⌣⏳

Gary Kidgell possesses a lifelong interest in all matters esoteric and has been a serious student of the Ancient Wisdom for over thirty years. He completed a Bachelor's Degree in Metaphysics through Claregate College under the auspices of Dr Douglas Baker and was then invited to become a course tutor and contributor. He is also the Director of Studies for the updated Claregate Metaphysics Correspondence Course.

Gary is a professional astrologer specialising in esoteric astrology and regularly holds astrology classes. He has lectured extensively throughout the UK and Europe on various esoteric subjects and has previously held the post of National Secretary for the Theosophical Society in Scotland.

Acknowledgements

The compilation of this book has been possible due to the assistance and inspiration of a number of friends and co-workers whom I have had the pleasure of encountering during the course of my spiritual endeavours.

Firstly, I am indebted to my principle mentor Dr Douglas Baker without whose profound spiritual insight the content of this book would not have been possible.

Next, I wish to convey my wholehearted gratitude to my long-standing friends and co-workers Alan Boxall and Richard Painter. Alan has been a constant source of support and encouragement both in respect of this book and our work together on behalf of the Claregate Group. Richard has tendered expert advice, personal insight and guidance in respect of the content and the layout of this book. Alan and Richard are both selfless, unsung, understated archetypal heroes who serve to cement a spiritually based group in true Aquarian fashion.

My thanks also to the Claregate Group as a whole and in particular to my greatly valued friends Paul Barker, Laurence Benson, Josh Brem-Wilson, Robert Brothers, Ted Capstick, David Clark, Marcus Hayward, Millo Magnocavallo, Scott Olsen, Gerald Parker, Mark Weight and Paul Wright. I thank each of them for the amity, spiritual advice and inspiration that they have provided me with over the years.

I extend my heartfelt thanks to Sue Darnell for her valuable editorial suggestions.

Finally, my deep appreciation is extended to everyone that I have engaged with in my life who have made this book possible and who are not mentioned above.

CONTENTS

FOREWORD

Gary Kidgell's express purpose in writing *The Inner Journey* was to produce a concise, yet thorough and practical manual that would 'assist and inspire' anyone treading the path of spiritual transformation. Solidly grounded in the eclectic Claregate path forged in the blood, sweat, tears and spiritual fire of his mentor, Dr. Douglas Baker, he has succeeded admirably! I am particularly impressed with the breadth of subjects covered, pertinent issues explained, and clarity of definitions of terminology. Always staying true to the various traditions, he nevertheless has followed the master word-crafter himself, Dr. Baker, expressing wherever possible the Ancient Wisdom in the language of the day.

This handy manual is also vintage Baker in drawing together some of our best esoteric forbears, including for example Blavatsky, Bailey, Leadbeater, Steiner, Socrates, Plato and Shankara. The setting is embedded in a rich and numinous collective background — fully reminiscent of the Elementary Ideas of Adolf Bastian, the Forms of Plato or the Archetypes of Carl Jung. This is further enriched, actually enflamed with the interplay of James Joyce, Joseph Campbell and the hero's journey, some Advaita Vedanta, an extremely relevant discussion of the Seven Rays and the aspirant's 'ray make-up', the importance of Esoteric Astrology, parallels of planetary and human chakras, purusha and prakriti, and the connection of Atman and Brahman in spiritual transformation.

Gary Kidgell has succeeded in producing a very practical and useful manual to assist anyone seeking guidance while treading the path of spiritual return or what the immortal Socrates referred to as 'the Jeweled Way.' This is nothing less than the Rainbow Path, the Antakarana that we consciously and purposely construct as we wind our way towards Samadhi, or cosmic conscious union with the Divine Source Itself. At the climactic summit the goal is attained: Atman becomes one with Brahman. 'I and the Father are One.' The base metal or lead of the aspirant's 'ego' is alchemically fused and transformed into the shining gold of the awakened Arhat. The Arthurian knight has discovered the Holy Grail. May you enjoy your journey, knowing you have wisely chosen Gary Kidgell, a well-trained and knowledgeable 'Sherpa-like guide' and his practical manual to 'assist and inspire' you along this difficult but life-rewarding transformative way.

Scott A. Olsen, Ph.D. Professor of Philosophy & Religion at the College of Central Florida, USA.

INTRODUCTION

I have written this book in the hope that it may assist and inspire you in your personal endeavours towards spiritual transformation. In seeking to achieve this, I offer a series of principles and techniques which are grounded in the teachings of Ancient Wisdom. These are also referred to as the Ageless Wisdom, the Perennial Wisdom or Wisdom Teachings.

The Ancient Wisdom is comprised of a vast body of esoteric teachings which describe both the constitution and the evolution of humanity and our universe. The timeless truths contained within the wisdom teachings underlie all esoteric practices, both historical and contemporary. The major religions of our world may be considered as attempts towards expressing these in accordance with a particular period in time, the associated culture and the temperament of the practitioners.

A recent expression of the Ancient Wisdom occurred in the latter part of the nineteenth, and into the twentieth Century. This occurred through the work of H.P. Blavatsky and various offshoots of the Theosophical Society, of which she was a co-founder. The principle and most noble aim of this organisation is to establish a 'universal brotherhood' of humanity without distinction of race, creed, sex, caste or colour. Underlying this objective, and at the very core of the wisdom teachings, is the descent of spirit into matter and the subsequent return to its origin. The latter is referred to as the 'spiritual path' or 'path of return'.

My own efforts towards treading the spiritual path began over thirty years ago. It was then that I awakened to the fact that there was considerably more to life than the treadmill of mundane, materialistic existence driven primarily by the pursuit of personal desires, whilst being underpinned by feelings of self-preservation. The 'spiritual awakening' that I underwent served as a source of incomparable joy and immense inspiration. A life bereft of meaning and direction had been instantly infused by the fires of spiritual aspiration and a pressing urgency to both connect with, and express the intent of the immortal aspect of my being.

My feelings here are best encapsulated by the opening verse and chorus to Friedrich Schiller's poem *Ode to Joy*. This classic work celebrates the brotherhood and unity of humanity. It is best known for its musical setting by Ludwig van Beethoven in the fourth and final movement of his *Ninth Symphony*:

Joy, beautiful spark of Gods,
Daughter of Elysium,
We enter, fire-imbibed,
Heavenly, thy sanctuary.
Thy magic powers re-unite
What custom's sword has divided
Beggars become Princes' brothers
Where thy gentle wing abides.
Be embraced, millions!
This kiss to the entire world!
Brothers, above the starry canopy
A loving father must dwell.

My feelings of elation and revelation coincided with those of responsibility, together with an urgency fuelled by the realisation that I must adequately equip myself towards treading the spiritual path. I also quickly discovered that whilst I had been subjected to an inflow of light and love, my personality was far from transformed. A considerable amount of hard work lay ahead as I sought to effect the archetypal process of spiritual transformation.

My experience of awakening also served to refine my moral conscience which, whilst not hitherto absent, suddenly became more exacting, judging me with enhanced rigour and censure. On occasions, I questioned whether I had not descended to a level of expression lower than that prior to the emergence of a spiritual purpose in my life. H.P. Blavatsky famously advised the earnest spiritual seeker that when one treads the path, 'all that is good and all that is evil surface'. Lower propensities and drives previously dormant in the unconscious psyche become vitalized by the inflow of spiritual energy. I learned that it is the purpose of one who treads the path to confront and overcome these as a means of ascending to higher levels of consciousness.

There were also times when, if not straying entirely from the spiritual path, and despite my earlier awakening, I sought refuge in the laybys of mundane existence. However, on each occasion my residence there quickly became uncomfortable as 'divine homesickness' intervened. This surfaced under the guise of dissatisfaction and disillusionment with my current state of affairs. Each time I would resume my treading of the path and the bitter-sweet experiences associated with this, in the knowledge that spiritual development occurs at deep levels of the psyche and is not necessarily apparent on the surface and, most importantly, that my endeavours here were of benefit not merely to myself, but to humanity as a whole.

In pursuit of my spiritual objectives I studied and sought to apply the tenets of various spiritual traditions. These included teachings contained within both the Western Mystery Tradition and those of Oriental origin. After my discovery and subsequent study of various theosophical teachings, I encountered the writings of Dr Douglas Baker with whom I studied for a Bachelor's Degree in Metaphysics through his Claregate College in Hertfordshire, England.

Douglas Baker considered it his life's work to offer the wisdom teachings to humanity in the 'language of the day'. After our meeting in 1991 he served as my mentor until his passing in November 2011. His voluminous work, and my memories relating to the various 'pearls of wisdom' which he personally offered to me, remain as a constant source of insight, inspiration and sustenance in my spiritual endeavours.

Upon completing the Claregate Degree Course in 1993 I was then invited to become a course tutor, this being a role, and an aspect of spiritual service, that I was delighted to assume. In 2010 I and Alan Boxall, a co-worker at Claregate, approached Douglas Baker and discussed with him the compilation of a new series of audio-visual courses as a means of updating and modernising the content of the existing Bachelor of Metaphysics Degree. He approved and commissioned these with the first new course being named *Foundations in Esoteric Studies*. As the title would suggest, this course is designed to offer the spiritual aspirant a solid grounding in the underlying principles and practices which relate to the process of spiritual transformation.

Whilst *The Inner Journey* is distinct from the Foundations in Esoteric Studies course, it is also designed to serve as a complementary text book in this respect. Towards these ends, I have included Douglas Baker's 'Seven Postulates of Ancient Wisdom'.[1] These appear in his classic work entitled *The Jewel in the Lotus*. The principles contained within the postulates provide a solid basis towards serious progress in one's spiritual endeavours. These 'building blocks' have been of great assistance to me in providing a key towards unlocking the timeless truths contained therein, whilst enabling me to apply these in my spiritual study and practice. I have tried, as far as possible, to avoid 'reciting' the postulates in a near-verbatim fashion, as they are outlined in *The Jewel in the Lotus*, by adding personal insights and applications of these where appropriate.

This work also espouses the related teachings and practices of the transpersonal psychologist Roberto Assagioli and the pioneering depth psychologist Carl Jung. I consider their works to be complementary to those of the wisdom teachings whilst also serving to augment their content in a manner which is applicable to life in our contemporary society. Jung's concept of archetypes, and their representation in the human psyche as symbols, is the most important 20th century contribution to the spiritual evolution of humanity.

Throughout this book you will observe that I offer interpretations of various hero myths as a means of symbolically depicting the archetypal challenges and rewards associated with the process of spiritual transformation. Myth plays a significant role in directing human consciousness inwards towards achieving what Jung referred to as 'wholeness'. When we undertake the evolutionary journey to the source of our being it is most helpful to be aware that the hero myths of our world depict what the great 20th century student of myth, Joseph Campbell, described as 'the hero's journey'. In engaging with the content of the hero myth, not only can we obtain an understanding of what may be described as the 'hero archetype', but we may also attune to the 'energy reservoirs' created by those members of humanity who have previously undertaken the inner journey.

I have compiled this work primarily with the intent of offering a solid theoretical foundation upon which to base your own understanding of the spiritual path, and to inform and assist you as to its challenges and rewards. In conjunction with this, I seek to offer a number of insights and practices designed to aid you towards accessing and expressing the energies and intent of the Soul or Higher Self. Essentially, my objective is to assist you towards becoming Soul-infused by utilising the energies of the inner worlds so that you may take your own steps towards effecting the archetypal process of spiritual transformation.

As a means of assisting you towards engaging with, assimilating and applying the content of this work in your own spiritual practice, may I state from the advice of my mentor and from subsequent personal experience that one generally reaps the greatest reward from the study of esoteric writings when the content is perused in a slow, careful and thoughtful manner. It is generally best to consider only a small amount of subject matter at any given time. You are advised to invest considerably more time pondering, reflecting upon, and contemplating the content than you do so in the actual act of reading.

Gary Kidgell

CHAPTER 1

THE INNER JOURNEY

T HE SITE OF DELPHI IS LOCATED ON THE SLOPES OF Mount Parnassus. This represented one of the most important sources of knowledge in Ancient Greece. Great and powerful individuals travelled from the farthest reaches of the known world, undertaking the long and often arduous journey, for the purpose of receiving the wisdom of Apollo, the Sun God. This was conveyed to them by the Pythia, the priestess of the temple, also known as the Delphic Oracle. Inscribed in the forecourt of the temple was the famous aphorism of 'Know Thyself'. The true meaning of this refers not merely to obtaining knowledge relating to the transient human personality with its physical body, feelings, emotions and thoughts, but rather towards gaining knowledge of the immortal and enduring aspect of our nature. This is the Soul or Higher Self, the instrument of the monad, our divine essence, whose purpose underlies our various activities in life whilst also constituting the very reason for our existence.

As a means of fulfilling the Delphic injunction we must tread the spiritual path which leads us from the transitory travails of material circumstance to the very source of our being. The pathway here is commonly symbolised as a mountainous ascent; we possess various options as to the means by which we may undertake our journey towards the summit. These options may be broadly categorised into three principle areas:

The first route that we may undertake involves us undergoing many lives, ambling along a pathway whose gentle gradient ensures that only a small degree of progress is made in each one as we spend numerous incarnations in the lowlands of our ordinary consciousness. The second option is where we pursue a somewhat steeper and therefore more demanding path as we seek to explore and express our creative potential. This ensures that we obtain a higher vantage point on the mountain. The third, and by far the most demanding route towards the summit is the symbolic scaling of the cliff-face whereby we undertake serious spiritual disciplines as a means of attaining our goal. Through us undertaking the latter option, the experiences and the lessons of many lives are compacted into a short few. As the symbolism here suggests, this is a most arduous and challenging process. However, the magnificent vistas, symbolising exalted states of consciousness which we may obtain here, render the effort worthwhile. In esoteric parlance this constitutes the 'path of discipleship'. A disciple may be described as an individual who undertakes serious spiritual disciplines.

Theosophical teachings, and the related writings of Alice Bailey, describe various stages of spiritual growth in terms of a series of initiations. These relate to vast expansions in our consciousness, accompanied by a markedly greater capacity towards carrying and expressing the divine life force. These enable us to express more successfully our portion of the evolutionary or divine plan. This is related to the spiritual intent of the great planetary consciousness within which we reside, and which the disciple seeks to align themselves to, through the undertaking of the required spiritual disciplines.[1]

The Greek philosopher Socrates described the path of spiritual transformation as the 'Jewelled Way', due to the fact that the route is ablaze with flashes of illumination. He referred to the immortal aspect of his being as his 'Daemon'. He would turn inward to consult his Daemon as a means of gaining insight and inspiration whilst ensuring that his course of action was in accord with that of the immortal aspect of his being. One of the principle objectives of this work is to assist you in developing sensitivity and receptivity to the Soul or Higher Self so that you too may be able to access its energies and express its purpose.

The mediaeval alchemists represented the archetypal process of spiritual transformation in their 'Great Work'. The culmination of their endeavours resulted in the 'base metal' of the transient, corruptible human personality being transformed into the shining, radiant, eternal gold of the Soul. Carl Jung was heavily influenced by the symbolism depicted in the various stages of the alchemical process together with the earlier related practices of Gnosticism, the symbolism of myth, and various other metaphysical teachings derived from both oriental and occidental sources.

Jung's fascination with alchemy developed after he received the text of *The Secret of the Golden Flower*, the Chinese version of alchemy, which his friend the sinologist Richard Wilhelm had sent to him in 1928. It was then that he realized that the alchemists, in outlining the content of their Great Work, were employing symbols for the purpose of describing the practice of spiritual transformation. Jung writes:

> *'The experiences of the alchemists were in a sense, my experience, and their world was my world... I had stumbled on the historical counterpart of my psychology of the unconscious. The possibility of a comparison with alchemy, and the uninterrupted intellectual chain back to Gnosticism, gave substance to my psychology.'* [2]

Jung described the process of spiritual transformation, and the means by which one may successfully achieve this, in his concept of Individuation, the objective here being that of Wholeness or Integration whereby the conscious and the unconscious elements of the human psyche, including the Soul, are unified. Jung believed that if one is sensitive and receptive to the unconscious, which, he stated,

Cadmus Asks the Delphic Oracle Where He Can Find his Sister, Europa, Hendrik Goltzius (Holland, Mülbracht [now Bracht-am-Niederrhein], 1558-1617). Holland, published 1615 Book: Metamorphoses by Ovid, book 3, plate 1

manifests within the human psyche in dream and fantasy, then one is able to align one's objectives and submit one's ego, together with its associated psychological drives, to a higher integrating factor. This is located within the unconscious or inner realms of the psyche. Jung referred to this as the Self. This equates with the Hindu concept of the Atman and in the wisdom teachings it relates particularly to the monad; however, we may also relate this to the Soul or Higher Self as the instrument of the monad.

Jung advanced the concept of 'archetypes' or 'divine ideas'. These had been introduced previously by Plato. It is the energies of the archetypes which govern and conduct the evolutionary process. Jung stated that they are vast reservoirs of psychic energy which form part of the collective unconscious. Jung informed us that archetypes manifest within the human psyche in symbolic form. The unconscious, which he described, possesses its own particular language whose characters are comprised of symbols. This has profound relevance for the individual who seeks to effect spiritual transformation. If we can recognise and interpret the language of the Soul which is conveyed to us in symbolic form, primarily through our dreams and the practice of meditation, we may become aware of the intent of the Soul. We can then attune to, and express, the energies of the archetypes as a means of achieving individuation. Such practice serves to develop the faculty of abstract thought or Higher Manas. This represents the current frontier in human consciousness

The Italian psychiatrist and visionary Roberto Assagioli described the archetypal process of spiritual transformation in his concept of Psychosynthesis. Assagioli was inspired by both eastern and western mysticism. A close friend of Alice Bailey, he wrote the forward to the Italian edition of her commentary on *The Yoga Sutras of Patanjali* entitled *The Light of the Soul*. Assagioli was also a friend of my mentor Douglas Baker.

As a means of effecting Psychosynthesis, which Assagioli also described as Self-realization, the individual seeks to purify and integrate their personality (consisting of the mental, astral and physical bodies) and its qualities and functions, into a coherent structure. They may then function as an effective spiritual instrument capable of expressing the purpose and intent of the Self. The existing personality, or ego- structure with its various attitudes, predispositions, desires and attachments is effectively de-constructed and thereafter assembled at a higher point of consciousness, with all that is irrelevant here being discarded. This enables the safe and successful infusion of spiritual energy to occur. Assagioli considered the correct application of the will to be instrumental in this process whereby the personal will is aligned to that of the Soul. When considered in the light of the perennial wisdom, and its teachings related to initiation, the objectives outlined in Assagioli's process of Psychosynthesis accord with those of Jung's concept of Individuation.

When we tread the spiritual path we respond to the promptings of our inner nature and awaken to our ultimate destiny. This is referred to as the 'pull of the monad'. Essentially, we are being prompted towards a return to the point of our divine origin. This occurs after the experience of what is described as 'divine unrest' where we are confronted by feelings of dissatisfaction and disillusionment with the transient affairs of the external world and its associated materialism. These aspects of our life, which previously formed the very basis of our efforts and endeavours, then fail to fascinate, motivate or sustain us. This state of affairs represents the stage of our lengthy evolutionary journey whereby we have reached saturation point in terms of our engagement and enmeshment with the material world. The juncture in human evolution has been reached where our desire nature, which has hitherto served a healthy purpose towards engaging spirit with matter, must now be transmuted into spiritual aspiration as our personality has to be reconstructed as a worthy repository of spiritual energy.

The archetypal process of spiritual transformation is symbolised in the various hero myths of our world. For example, The Twelve Labours of Hercules represents the archetypal challenges and rewards associated with incarnation in the twelve astrological signs as the Soul traverses the round of the zodiac for the final time, prior to attaining liberation from the Wheel of Rebirth. Jason ventures forth in pursuit of the Golden Fleece which symbolises the spiritual gold of the alchemists. This may only be obtained after the base metal of the human personality has undergone the necessary transformation towards such ends. The challenges associated with this process are symbolised by his various exploits. In their quest for the Grail the knights of Camelot undergo many tests and trials in the Forest Adventurous before they may prove themselves worthy to attain the miraculous receptacle of divine energy, which symbolises the Soul.

The great 20th century mythologist Joseph Campbell embraced Jung's theories relating to the structure of the human psyche. This included Jung's concept of the archetypes as divine ideas. Campbell illustrated how the various myths of our world illustrate a single story of humanity and its strivings towards realising its divine potential. He emphasised that every myth is 'psychologically symbolic' and that its narratives and images are not to be assumed as literal, but rather as metaphors.

Campbell adopted a comparative approach towards interpreting the symbolism of myth by perceiving a common pattern underlying its narrative elements. He described this as 'the hero's journey', a term which he borrowed from the novelist James Joyce who used this in his book, *Finnegan's Wake*. In his classic work, *The Hero with a Thousand Faces*, Campbell illustrates how the mythological hero responds to what he describes as 'the call to adventure'. Thereafter, the hero ventures forth into distant and dangerous lands that symbolise the inner worlds, realms of the unconscious that must be explored. It is here that he encounters various tests and trials which determine his right to proceed further and ultimately to attain his goal. Campbell demonstrates how the hero must leave behind the entanglements of everyday life in pursuit of spiritual initiation, and how once this has been attained he must then return to the rank and file of humanity as a 'transfigured' individual who offers the lessons of his experience to others as an act of service. Campbell writes:

> '*A hero ventures forth from the world of common day into a region of supernatural wonder: fabulous forces are there encountered and a decisive victory is won: the hero comes back from this mysterious adventure with the power to bestow boons on his fellow men.*'[3]

We witness parallels with the hero's journey of Campbell and the various descriptions of the spiritual path which I have presented in this Chapter. They are all descriptive of the same process and goal as outlined in the wisdom teachings. When we tread the path, regardless of the particular model or methodology which we embrace, we are essentially pursuing the same objective of connecting with and expressing our innate spirituality whereby we may fulfil our potential as part of an evolutionary plan or design.

CHAPTER 2

PRINCIPLES OF THE WISDOM TEACHINGS

IF WE ARE TO ACHIEVE ANY SERIOUS MEASURE OF success in treading the spiritual path, whereby we may ascend the symbolic mountain of initiation, then we must take sufficient steps in preparing for such a task. A mountaineer would wish to undertake adequate preparation before embarking upon their ascent towards a most challenging summit. They would ensure that they had undertaken the requisite physical training, that they possessed the correct equipment, were sufficiently aware of the nature of the terrain, the expectant climatic conditions which are to confront them, and so on.

Similarly, when we tread the path we must be adequately equipped in that we should possess the necessary knowledge in terms of that which we are actually seeking to achieve. It is essential that we are aware of the disciplines which we must undertake, and their resultant effects, as we endeavour to connect with and express the intent of the Soul. It is imperative that we possess an understanding of the dynamics of our psyche and of our relationship to the subjective realms of consciousness. We must ally the factor of self-discipline to our spiritual aspiration as a means of enabling us to persist in our endeavours as we tread the razor-edged path between the outer and inner worlds.

When we embark upon the process of spiritual transformation we must realise that *the journey is the goal*. It is the experiences that we undergo in traversing the 'jewelled way' which lead to expansions in consciousness and in our level of being. The symbolic lotus petals of the Soul are unfolded by means of our genuine efforts towards connecting with the immortal aspect of our being, and in expressing its energies and qualities.

As a means of equipping ourselves towards treading the path, it is most helpful to be aware of certain fundamental principles. These serve as a key towards unlocking the timeless truths found within the perennial wisdom whereby we may derive a degree of understanding that enables us to apply these to our spiritual practice, and in our daily lives. In his classic work *The Jewel in the Lotus*[1] Douglas Baker lists seven postulates of the Ancient Wisdom. These may be summarised as follows:

1. All things are filled with life, from the tiniest atom to the greatest galaxy;

2. All things live within the body of a greater being;

3. All things are made in the image of the one in whom they live and move and have their being;

4. There is a continuum which links all living things together so that the smallest cell does not pulsate without its effects being felt in the furthest reaches of the solar system;

5. Our universe is constructed out of energies which resonate to seven qualities;

6. The solidity and tangibility of the material world is an illusion; it is part of maya. All is energy manifesting as Fire and Form. Energy and matter are interchangeable;

7. There is no death, only change of state. Birth and Rebirth are endless until karma is satisfied, and then reincarnation ceases.

Mountains: Symbols of Initiation

It is most helpful to take time in considering the foregoing principles. The postulates can assist you greatly towards establishing a solid basis towards an in-depth study and application of the esoteric. It will be most beneficial if you can, through a process of pondering and contemplation, identify with the content of these postulates whilst recognising these in your daily life. This can serve to promote expansions in your consciousness and level of being.

The postulates which are presented in this work, in varying order from the above, are interrelated. An understanding of the first one, relating to the living nature of our universe, leads to a clearer understanding of those which follow.

CHAPTER 3

A CONSCIOUS LIVING UNIVERSE

THE FIRST POSTULATE OF THE ANCIENT WISDOM informs us that 'all things are filled with life, from the tiniest atom to the greatest galaxy'.

The wisdom teachings consider our universe to be a conscious, living being, rather than adopting the assertions of materialistic science which believes it to be comprised of inert matter and empty space. The universal mind is a stupendous and immeasurably vast entity which is infinitely creative, possesses synchronistic qualities, and is in a continuous state of evolution. The sum total of the divine consciousness of the universal mind is comprised of the Seven Rays and their respective energies (the Seven Rays are discussed in Chapter 10). Everything contained within our universe, from the tiniest atom to the greatest galaxy, receives and responds to its energies whilst contributing to its overall functioning as part of a vast evolutionary tapestry of interconnectedness.

All matter contained within our universe is infused by the energy and qualities of an underlying subjective component THE ONE LIFE. This causal aspect of the universe gives coherence and structure to all forms found within creation. It is important for the spiritual seeker to be aware that the rich diversity of forms, which the divine life assumes, function as vehicles by which aspects of that divine life (monads) at varying stages of their lengthy evolutionary sojourn, may develop and express hitherto latent qualities.

An understanding of this profound esoteric truth has been demonstrated in various religious and mystical and esoteric doctrines. The teachings of Advaita Vedanta inform us that the entire universe is a sentient living being. We are advised here that the formless, impersonal divine reality known as Brahman[1] is both transcendent of, yet also immanent within, all forms. This is beautifully encapsulated in the famous quote from the Bhagavad Gita delivered by Krishna to Arjuna: *Having pervaded the universe with a fragment of myself I remain.*[2]

In her classic work *The Secret Doctrine*, H.P. Blavatsky employed the term 'hylozoism' to describe the infusion of matter with Life.[3] The concept of hylozoism is demonstrated by the pantheistic nature of the Hindu religion as well as by cultures including the American Indian, African, Ancient Middle Eastern, Japanese Shinto and various pagan traditions here in the west. This principle was also embraced by pre-Socratic philosophers of Ancient Greece including Thales, Anaximenes and Democritus. Prior to them, it was espoused by Zarathustra the founder of the Zoroastrian religion. Notable exponents of hylozoism during the Renaissance include the great mediaeval alchemist and physician Paracelsus and the so-called Christian heretic Giordano Bruno.

The principle of hylozoism is symbolically depicted in various creation myths, where many traditions state how creation occurs due to the sacrificial death of a primordial being. This is demonstrated in the Chinese myth relating to the primordial being Pan Gu which describes how our world was created: Pan Gu was the offspring of the two cosmic forces Yin and Yang which interact to produce the universe, and are viewed as complementary and mutually dependant. Out of the formless chaos a vast primordial egg coalesced from which Pan Gu came into being. Within this egg he grew for eighteen thousand years before it split open; the light, clear parts of the egg then rose to form the heavens whilst the heavy, opaque parts sank to form the Earth. Pan Gu stood up and held the heavens and the Earth apart growing taller by ten feet a day for another eighteen thousand years until they solidified into their present positions.

The weary God then lay down to rest before dying. We are informed that his breath became wind and cloud, his voice thunder, his left eye the Sun, his right eye the Moon, his hair and whiskers the stars in the sky whilst his limbs became pillars which formed the four corners of the Earth. The other parts of his body became the various elements that comprise the Earth, including mountains, rivers, plants, trees, metals, gems and rocks. His sweat was transformed into rain and dew. One version of this myth states that the parasites on his body became the ancestors of humanity.

Similarly, in one of the hymns of the *Rig Veda* we find the sacrifice of the primeval giant Purusha (the Sanskrit word for spirit) whereby all of the entities of the universe are produced from his dismembered body including the Vedic gods, the atmosphere, heaven and Earth, humanity and the animals. The Indian teachings of Jainism, Sankyha and Yoga each describe how purusha infuses prakriti (matter). This concept was developed further by the teachings of Advaita Vedanta which, as we have seen, state that the divine life, known as Brahman, is both transcendent of, yet also immanent within all forms.

These, and many other creation myths devised by the ancients, symbolise the divine life projecting aspects of itself downwards into matter thereby giving rise to our physical world. It is by virtue of the creation of the physical world that the monads, or sparks of the divine, may then adopt various corporeal forms as a means of developing and expressing hitherto latent spiritual qualities.

In essence we are monads, indivisible sparks of The One Flame Divine. This great spiritual entity is commonly referred to as the Solar Logos. Our entire solar system is viewed as a manifestation of this divine being. As a means of effecting spiritual growth the Solar Logos projects its component parts down the various planes of consciousness, ranging from the spiritual to the dense physical, as part of a vast evolutionary process. The monads therefore embark upon a

The Return of the Prodigal Son by Rembrandt (1642) Teylors Museum, Haarlem.

long evolutionary journey involving a descent into the various planes of existence upon what is referred to as the involutionary arc which culminates in expression, via a group-soul, in the mineral kingdom.

Then the ascent begins on the evolutionary arc through group-souls in the plant, and then the animal kingdom, before individualisation occurs as the monad enters the human kingdom. This is followed by expression in myriad human forms in different cultures and races before one eventually embarks upon the spiritual path. Upon successfully traversing the path of return one is then liberated from the Wheel of Rebirth and may eventually return to the great solar being from whence one came having completed one's part in the evolutionary plan for our solar system.

The Solar Logos can only evolve through the evolution of its component parts; each and every monad undertakes the descent into matter and subsequent return to source. This process is symbolically depicted in the Biblical parable of The Return of the Prodigal Son. The objective of the monad's lengthy evolutionary sojourn is to acquire *spiritual staying power*. This relates to its ability to radiate and express its qualities amidst the constraints of the planes of consciousness below it, of which the densest, and most challenging, is the physical. H.P. Blavatsky described the objective of reincarnation upon the Wheel of Rebirth as follows:

> *'Try to imagine a 'Spirit', a celestial being, whether we call it by one name or another, divine in its essential nature, yet not pure enough to be one with the ALL, and having, in order to achieve this, so to purify its nature as to finally gain that goal. It can do so only by passing 'individually' and 'personally', i.e. spiritually and physically, through every experience and feeling that exists in the manifold or differentiated universe. It has, therefore, after having gained such experience in the lower kingdoms, and having ascended higher and higher with every rung on the ladder of being, to pass through every experience on the human planes.'*[4]

The teachings of Alice Bailey employ the terms Life, Quality and Appearance to describe the interplay between spirit and matter, the word 'Life' here meaning the monad or divine essence, 'Appearance' relating to the form which it temporarily inhabits. 'Quality' describes the extent to which the indwelling life, through its instrument the Soul, can express its intent through the form. When we tread the path we must seek to develop and express our spirituality thus enabling the indwelling life, or monad, to demonstrate such quality despite the many challenges and constrictions imposed by the form within which it is temporarily encased. It is a very useful exercise for anyone who wishes to grasp the essence of the principle of hylozoism to take the time in their life to observe the various forms contained within our world, and, in each case, to consider the ability of the indwelling life towards expressing its quality despite the constraints to which it is subjected. It is worth noting in this respect that the extent to which we may apprehend such quality being demonstrated through another life form is determined by the extent to which our own particular quality is present.

It is important to be aware that the theory of hylozoism also applies at subjective levels of the human psyche. Thoughts are living things, they are elemental structures born within the mental body in the subtle region surrounding the mental counterpart of the pineal gland. Blavatsky labelled this the 'uterus of the brain'. Through spiritual practices such as meditation, creative visualisation and guided imagery we are able to create very potent, and most importantly, images linked to our consciousness at subjective levels. These provide a means by which the Soul may communicate with us by adopting and energising thus forming the basis of creative visualisation as a means of enabling us to access energy and meaning from within and where we may engage in symbolic dialogue with the Soul.

Carl Jung illustrated how archetypes are represented within the human psyche as symbols. We may consider these as living in that they offer us dynamic, subjective meaning whilst being laden with energy. The study and interpretation of symbolism assists us towards developing the faculty of abstract thought, or Higher Manas. By developing this faculty we build a bridge to the higher planes of consciousness where the Soul resides enabling the Higher Self to infuse us with its energies and qualities. This is referred to as the antakarana or rainbow bridge (the antakarana serves to link Soul and personality. It is discussed in Chapter 17).

We may create an image for the Soul in meditation such as that of a lotus flower, a five-pointed star, an angelic figure, an inner sage or indeed any image which we deem to be appropriate in terms of symbolising the indwelling immortal aspect of our being. In doing this we are creating a reservoir of spiritual energy which we may draw upon for sustenance in our spiritual endeavours and in times of stress in our life with this occurring as a natural consequence of us treading the path.

CHAPTER 4

LIFE WITHIN LIFE

IN CONSIDERING THE FIRST POSTULATE OF THE Ancient Wisdom we established that our universe is a sentient, living being whereby the One Divine Life is both transcendent and also immanent. It is therefore logical for us to assume that the principle of hylozoism applies to all forms contained within our universe, and therefore not only to the atom and the sub-atomic structures that comprise it, or to human beings, but rather it extends also to the considerably greater structures found within our universe including those of a planet, a solar system and beyond.

The second postulate of the Ancient Wisdom advises us that 'all things live within the body of a greater being'.

Atoms are comprised of sub-atomic particles. They reside within the body of the molecule with these living structures forming part of the body of a greater being which, in this case, is the tissue cell or unicellular organism. Cells are aggregated to form considerably greater structures throughout nature, up to and including the human form. Similarly, collective groups of humanity are part of what are referred to as Sub-Races which in turn are part of Root-Races. These represent components of humanity itself. The terms 'Sub' and 'Root Race' refer to a particular group of humans who are assembled together for the objective of developing and expressing a certain evolutionary quality.

We are analogous to cells residing within humanity which itself is a great entity. Humanity may be viewed as a leviathan whereby the various Root Races represent chakras or force centres. Our present Root Race, the Aryan, is the throat chakra of this great life. The previous Atlantean Root Race represented the solar plexus centre, and the Root Race prior to this, the Lemurian, signified the sacral centre. Similarly, the respective Root Races here emphasised the opening of these particular chakras within the human microcosm.

Humanity itself exists as a chakra within the consciousness of a great being which operates through our planet, referred to as the Planetary Logos. The scientist James Lovelock used the term 'Gaia' to describe the living nature of our planet, having taken this name from the goddess of Greek mythology who personified the Earth. Humanity is described as the throat centre of the Earth. The head centre of the Planetary Logos is Shamballa, this being the point from where the will of the divine is directed, the legendary abode in Central Asia where the hierarchy of spiritual masters are said to reside. It is they who represent the heart centre of the planetary life whereby they receive the logoic impulse of love and transmit this to Earth. The lower kingdoms of nature—mineral, plant and animal—represent the planetary centres, the base of the spine, the sacral and the solar plexus respectively.

Our planet itself is a chakra within the body of the Solar Logos. The solar being is, in turn, the heart chakra within an immense cosmic entity referred to as The One About Whom Naught May Be Said which is comprised of seven solar systems. Due to its location as the heart centre within The One the dominant force within our solar system, and the key towards spiritual development and growth, is that of LOVE. This relates to the Second Ray of Love-Wisdom, one of the seven great universal builders, whose qualities are those of Love Wisely Applied and Wisdom-Lovingly Applied.

The essence of this postulate is that each entity, regardless of its size, is alive and residing within the body of a greater being upon the evolutionary scale. In each instance the structures that exist within the greater being contribute towards the functioning of their host, whilst also being subject to their host's superior rhythms and impulses.

Spiritual development consists of the progressive opening of the chakras with the unfolding of their petals representing what may be referred to as 'signposts on the path'. When we seek spiritual transformation there is a transfer of energy to be achieved between the lower chakras and their higher counterparts. This is paralleled by the energies of the Soul being increasingly drawn into our aura through the practice of spiritual disciplines.

As we strive towards spiritual expression and growth so we contribute to the evolution of the planetary and solar beings of which we are a part, who are undergoing the self-same process at a considerably higher level of the evolutionary scale. The process of yoga is taking place at human, planetary and solar levels and indeed beyond these, within the body of The One About Whom Naught May Be Said. This is in accordance with the Law of Correspondence which is reflected in the Hermetic axiom of 'As Above, So Below'.

Douglas Baker writes:

'We must remember that we mirror, in our own journey, that taken by the Solar Logos. His manifestation is through three outpourings of Fire.[1] Eventually, He slowly withdraws these into Himself at the end of the mahamanvantara[2] and blazes into a supernova. In microcosm, we do the same and must withdraw all Fires into the head. There are safe and effective pathways for these energies and, in general, they move always upwards from chakras below the level of the diaphragm to chakras above the diaphragm.'[3]

The passage of fire here moves from lower chakras to their higher counterparts as follows:

Base of Spine to Crown Chakra
Sacral Chakra to Throat Chakra
Solar Plexus Chakra to Heart Chakra
Heart Chakra to Brow Chakra
Throat Chakra to Alta Major Chakra

The alta major chakra is located at the base of the skull. This is brought into activity in the latter stages of the spiritual path through service to humanity. Its interaction with the brow and head chakras (which are stimulated through focus of the mind and meditation respectively) creates a vortex of energy leading to the emergence and opening of the Third Eye.

Astrology, and particularly esoteric astrology, provides us with an understanding of the immense beings or lives which comprise the universal consciousness. Douglas Baker described astrology as a study of the *'physiology of our universe'*. Immense beings operate and interact through the zodiacal constellations and influence human affairs, both individually and collectively, in accordance with this postulate and its antecedent—the principle of hylozoism.

Through an understanding of Esoteric Astrology we are offered a means of attuning to requirements of the living, dynamic universe of which we are an integral part. The astrological natal chart, when considered from an esoteric perspective, may be viewed as a mandala. It is a symbolic representation of our route towards what Jung described as Individuation whereby the conscious and the unconscious aspects of the human psyche are unified. It is our own map of the psyche which offers us a route towards the attainment of Wholeness, or Psychosynthesis. The natal chart is comprised of a set of celestial instructions which can assist us towards realising our innate spiritual potential, this in accord with the intent of the great beings, and indeed the vast universal consciousness within which we reside.

The Wheel of the zodiac plays a central role throughout the entire journey of the Soul upon the Wheel of Rebirth. Astrology and the great universal law of karma determine the circumstances of each incarnation. In esoteric astrology the Three Crosses associated with the quadruplicities of astrology—Cardinal, Fixed and Mutable—

indicate the three fundamental stages of the Soul's journey through matter. The experiences of humanity upon the *Mutable Cross* provide diverse forms of experience propelled by the factor of desire. This serves towards opening the symbolic knowledge petals of the Soul. It is upon the *Fixed Cross* that one experiences the pull of the instincts and desires on the one hand, and the archetypal energies which seek to drive them towards the Fifth Kingdom of Souls on the other. Throughout this part of the Soul's evolutionary sojourn desire is transmuted into spiritual aspiration. The experiences here stimulate the symbolic Love Petals of the Egoic Lotus. The final series of incarnations of the Soul upon the *Cardinal Cross* serve to unfold the symbolic Sacrifice Petals providing opportunities towards performing great acts of personal sacrifice in service to humanity and the planet itself. It is the culmination of one's endeavours here that results in the higher initiations and what the Hindus call 'Moksha' meaning release from the Wheel of Rebirth.[4]

The Soul and the Greater Consciousness Within Which It Resides

It is now appropriate to consider a very important implication relating to the second postulate namely that 'the Soul of an entity is the consciousness of the one in which it lives and moves and has its being'. Human cells are alive and sentient and their aggregation constitutes their human host. The Soul of each cell is an aspect of the relatively immense consciousness of the one in whom they live and move and have their being. Each individual cell reflects certain aspects of the greater being within which it resides, whilst it also contributes towards the functioning of its host.

Similarly, the Soul of one particular human being and that of another are one and the same in that they are aspects of the consciousness of the greater being in which they reside, the Planetary Logos. The consciousness of this greater being, which is seeking evolutionary growth through our planet, is comprised of the myriad Souls which are operating through the various forms found on Earth. This provides insight and meaning to the statement that my Soul and your Soul are one and the same. The Soul of each and every member of the human kingdom seeks to direct its personality, as its medium of expression in the lower worlds, towards the fulfilment of its purpose, with this being in alignment to that of the greater being within which it resides.

When we undertake various forms of spiritual development, we are essentially seeking to fashion our personality into an effective spiritual instrument whereby we are able to fulfil the objectives of the Soul. Through undertaking the practices and disciplines associated with the treading of the path, and by eliminating feelings and perceptions of separateness, we may become conscious of the greater being within which we reside whereby we are rendered eligible to share in its energies and powers via our own Soul or Higher Self.

We must be aware that our lives occur within the context of a long series where the Soul is gradually moulding the personality into an effective instrument of spiritual expression. When we adopt the disciplines of the path we are aligning our intent to that of the Higher Self. Douglas Baker would often state that for every step we take towards the Soul, it will take two steps towards us!

When we sense our connection with the enduring and immortal aspect of our being and take steps towards linking our consciousness to the Soul, our progress towards spiritual growth is greatly accelerated leading to vast expansions in consciousness in the latter stages. Throughout this process we are becoming increasing aligned to the intent of the Planetary Logos, the one in whom we live and move and have our being.

Our ability to connect with the Soul and therefore to the intent of the Planetary Logos is greatly assisted by the process of yoga which is related to various spiritual disciplines that originated in India. Yogic practices enable one to attain what the Hindus refer to as Samadhi. In Zen Buddhism this is described as Satori whilst in the west it is commonly known as Cosmic Consciousness. This is the state of being where one experiences omniscience, omnipotence and omni-presence due to one's ability to yoke one's consciousness to that of the greater entity within which one resides.[5] Such exalted states of being, including those described in the higher initiations of the wisdom teachings, offer one perception of the intent of the greater entity within which they exist whereby this may then be conveyed to humanity as a means of assisting in implementing the divine plan.

This postulate, and its implications, emphasises the need for humanity to realise the importance of mutual cooperation and group relationships. This is especially so as we have now entered the astrological Age of Aquarius, the sign of the water-bearer who is pouring out the symbolic waters of knowledge for the purpose of quenching the thirst of the spiritual seeker. In esoteric astrology Aquarius, its planetary ruler Jupiter, and the 11th house of the natal chart rule group associations. These provide us with an opportunity to obtain expansions in our consciousness. This astrological archetype exhorts humanity, and especially those who are treading the path, to develop the ability towards working in association with others in pursuit of collective objectives in accordance with the keynote of the prevailing astrological age.

CHAPTER 5

THE WHEEL OF REBIRTH

POSTULATE SEVEN OF THE ANCIENT WISDOM STATES that '...there is no death only change of state. Birth and rebirth are endless until karma is satisfied, and then reincarnation ceases'. We shall explore the nature of this postulate in the following three chapters.

Life and death occur as part of a cyclical process. In commenting upon the symbolism that is conveyed by the Wheel of Rebirth, Douglas Baker writes:

'Our various lives are seen as spokes on a wheel. Each spoke, in turn, bears the whole of the Soul's forward urge, even if for a brief period. Between lives, the consciousness returns to the hub of the wheel where the movement hardly exists at all and where there is rest and where all the spokes of the lives past, present and future have their anchor and where memory of them is restored.

*Eventually, we remain at the centre of the wheel, freed from rebirth,
and then we see the wheel not as the instrument of almost
unendurable torture, but as a flower of the Soul.*'[1]

In classical myth the ruler of the Olympian pantheon Zeus takes pity
upon the errant King Ixion by introducing him at the table of the gods.
Rather than displaying gratitude, Ixion develops a passion for Hera,
the wife of Zeus. The king of the gods discovers the lustful intent of
his guest and foils this by creating a cloud which resembles Hera.
Ixion couples with the cloud named Nephele. Some mythological
accounts state that this gave rise to the race of Centaurs, whilst other
accounts state that the union of Ixion and Nephele created a son
named Centaurus who mated with the mares who inhabited the
mountains and forests of Magnesia, thus creating the savage half-man,
half-horse race. Zeus then expelled Ixion from Mount Olympus by
blasting him with a thunderbolt. He ordered Hermes, the messenger
of the Gods, to bind Ixion to a fiery wheel which rolled unceasingly
through the underworld.

   In considering the symbolism of this myth, Zeus represents the
divine principle within humanity which is seeking development and
expression within the womb of creation, which is symbolised by his
consort Hera. The punishment of Ixion illustrates both the futility and
the consequences for those members of humanity who are unwilling
to transcend their instinctual and desire-driven tendencies. They are
effectively bound to what Douglas Baker describes as '*an instrument
of almost unendurable torture*'. The fiery passions and instincts of such
individuals serve to continually generate karma which shackles them
to the Wheel of Rebirth and to the energies of the lower realms of the
unconscious. One thereby endures a self-perpetuating hell in that one's
pursuit of self-gratification offers no satisfaction of an enduring nature
as one's endeavours relate entirely to that which is transient.

   Zeus creates a cloud to resemble Hera. The symbolism of the cloud
is most appropriate as a representation of *maya* or illusion due to its
especially ephemeral qualities. Ixion mates with the cloud which leads
to the creation of the Centaurs whose half-human, half-animal nature
represents the hegemony of the instincts at the expense of spiritual

Punishment of Ixion- Fresco from the picture gallery of House of the Vettii in Pompeii

expression. In esoteric astrology, clouds are ruled by the sign of Cancer, its ruling planet Neptune and the 4th house of the natal chart. This astrological archetype also governs both maya and the human imagination. The combination of these is instrumental in generating human desire.

The archetypal energies of each astrological sign can be expressed in positive ways which assist the process of evolution, and in negative ways whereby spirit becomes more closely entangled in matter and all that this entails. Cancer rules the mothering principle and therefore the capacity to give birth. Included here is the giving of birth to creative ideas. When treading the path we may use the imagination as part of the process of creating 'seed thoughts' in meditation which assist us in constructing the antakarana which links the Soul and personality. The foregoing matters are especially applicable to those who are born with Cancer on the Ascendant[2] in the natal chart but the expression of the gifts and the overcoming of the challenges associated with this astrological archetype are relevant to us all as we tread the path. The creation of seed thoughts assists us towards becoming Soul-infused whilst we also support humanity here by creating structures at the mental level which aid the process of evolution. As P. B. Shelley states in his famous work *The Poet's Dream*:

> '*But from these create he can, forms more real than living man, nurslings of immortality.*'

We are presented with choices as we traverse the Wheel of Rebirth. In treading the path, by undertaking the associated practices and disciplines, the Wheel of Rebirth serves its intended purpose towards unfolding the flower of the Soul. However, if we are intent upon utilising the realms of the goddess solely towards self-gratification, then we are inexorably bound Ixion-like to the wheel which Buddhist teachings depict as being turned by the pig, the bird and the snake which symbolise ignorance, attachment and aversion respectively.

CHAPTER 6

THE ESOTERIC HUMAN CONSTITUTION

IN OUR CONSIDERATION OF POSTULATE SEVEN, FOR the purpose of gaining an appreciation of its content, it is appropriate to outline the esoteric human constitution. The diagram on page 42 illustrates the planes of consciousness ranging from the physical to the monadic together with the various constituents of the human constitution. It is important to be aware that this is merely a two-dimensional representation of a multi-dimensional creation and also that the planes depicted here interpenetrate.

Firstly, we shall consider the human personality and its three vehicles—the physical, astral and mental bodies. Each and every Soul in incarnation possesses a physical body which is comprised of solid, liquid and gaseous substance derived from the Earth. These are the three lowest levels, or sub-planes, of the physical plane. Ninety-nine percent of the mass of the physical body is comprised of the six elements oxygen, carbon, hydrogen, nitrogen, calcium, and

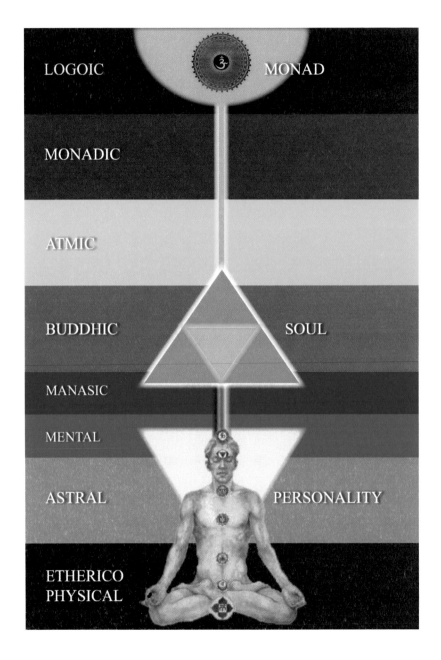

LOGOIC   MONAD

MONADIC

ATMIC

BUDDHIC   SOUL

MANASIC

MENTAL

ASTRAL   PERSONALITY

ETHERICO
PHYSICAL

The Planes of Consciousness

phosphorus whilst approximately 0.85 percent is composed of another five elements: potassium, sulphur, sodium, chlorine, and magnesium. The small remaining percentage is constituted of trace elements.

The physical body possesses an etheric counterpart which is comprised of the upper four of the seven sub-planes of the physical plane. The etheric body acts as a physiological unit and serves as a matrix to the development of the physical body. The etheric body is comprised of fine wire-like, scintillating threads which are referred to as nadis. The etheric chakras are found at major points where groups of these nadis intersect.

The etheric body serves to vitalise the nervous system whilst it provides the solid, liquid and gaseous components of the physical body with an energy that is considerably more subtle and refined than that derived from food metabolism. This energy is known as prana, which is stored in vitality globules which are comprised of seven anu or ultimate atoms (the anu is discussed in Chapter 9) linked together by prana, which is found in the sunlit atmosphere. Prana is ingested primarily through our respiratory system. The vitality globules break down inside the etheric body whereby it is channelled via the nadis into the chakras.

At a more subtle level than the etheric, we find the astral body. This provides the means by which we feel and express our emotions. The astral body is derived from the emotional substance of the astral world. When any human being or creature experiences feeling, they create substance of an astral denseness in the astral world by virtue of their astral body which serves as their vehicle of consciousness in this realm of being.

The astral body leaves the physical body in the sleep state where it functions in the astral world and the phenomenon of out-of-body and near-death-experiences are related to the separation of the astral body from the physical body. The energies of the astral plane are focussed upon the solar plexus chakra located in the abdomen region. The astral body synthesises these forces whereby we may use them effectively either towards personal ends, including the pursuit of our many varied desires, or for the purpose of assisting the evolutionary process by various forms of creative and spiritual expression. Spiritual development is closely related to our ability to exert control over the astral body and the various desires which originate here.

The last of the personality bodies is the most subtle. This is the mental body which is derived from the substance of the mental world comprised of the four lowest of the mental sub-planes. The mental body generates thoughts on a constant basis. The yoga teachings inform us of how the mind is in a state of perpetual agitation in that it continually assumes the forms and colours of everything that is presented to it by the senses, our imagination, our emotions and memory. It is a most challenging matter when we try to focus on a single image or thought. Almost immediately, associated thoughts occur due to the constant activity of the mind. In Buddhism the undisciplined mind is metaphorically described as 'the chattering monkey' due to its restless and unsettled nature. Akin to a monkey jumping from one branch of a tree to another, the mind is in constant movement. In the vast majority of humanity most of its thoughts are driven by the astral body as a means of satisfying its various desires. In the Hindu teachings this is referred to as kama-manas, meaning 'mind contaminated by desire'.

The analogy of a pond being rippled by the wind is a metaphor employed by the Advaita Vedanta teachings to describe the machinations of the mind and its fascination with the objects of the outer world which prevent one from perceiving the underlying divine reality. When the wind causes ripples in the water, only broken images of the objects surrounding the pond can be seen as reflections. However, if the water is stilled then the image of the objects surrounding the pond can be perceived in its entirety. One may also then see what is below the surface of the pond. The yoga teachings advise us that we are in essence an aspect of Brahman, the divine transcendent reality. However, we incorrectly identify with the splintered images flickering on the pond's surface, yet when we practise meditation, in accordance with the teachings of yoga we are trying to still the waters of the pond so that we may discover ways to perceive our essence.

The personality is the instrument of the Soul. It is chosen as a means of expressing the objectives of the Soul in the lower worlds so that it may contribute to its evolution. The Latin word 'persona' describes the mask worn by Ancient Greek and Roman actors indicating the role that they happened to be playing. This, of course, is an apt description for the Soul's mechanism. Indeed the diverse array of material forms contained in our world may be considered as masks that obscure the one divine life that is both immanent, yet also transcendent of its own creation.

It is important to bear in mind that each of us, as human personalities, has a unique purpose to fulfil in accordance with the objectives of the Soul. By treading the path we undertake certain spiritual disciplines and practices as a means of purifying and integrating the components of our personality, the physical, astral and mental bodies together with all of our qualities and functions, so that we may be safely and successfully infused with the energies of the Soul. As we have seen, this is the process which Assagioli described as Psychosynthesis and which Jung labelled Individuation. Upon attaining such a state of being we may then safely and successfully express the intent of the Higher Self. The spiritual practices here include Study of the wisdom teachings, the regular practice of Meditation, and the rendering of acts of Service to humanity and/or to the planet in general.

Secondly, we must now consider the immortal and enduring part of the human constitution whose purpose is the very reason for the existence of the personality. The Soul or Higher Self is a reflection of its father in heaven, the monad, and serves as its instrument upon the planes below it. Due to the purity of its vibration the monad cannot descend beneath its own level of being; it therefore adopts the Soul as its mechanism of expression so that it may function upon the planes of consciousness below its own.

The Soul exists as a means of attaining a complete form of consciousness whereby it can respond to every vibration of life that surrounds it on each and every level of existence. This process involves a series of many lives in human form upon the Wheel of Rebirth. It is only upon successfully learning every experience that life in human form has to offer that we are freed from the need to incarnate. We are then released from the Wheel of Rebirth which has served its purpose to unfold the flower of the Soul thus enabling the monad to obtain its objective during its long evolutionary sojourn of acquiring spiritual staying power.

The eminent Theosophist Annie Besant compared the succession of personalities which the Soul adopts to leaves upon a tree. She describes the Soul as:

> *'The immortal tree that puts out all these personalities as leaves, to last through the spring, summer and autumn of human life. All that the leaves take in and assimilate enriches the sap that courses through their veins, and in the autumn this is withdrawn into the parent-trunk, and the dry leaf falls and perishes.'*[1]

The Soul operates upon the levels or planes of consciousness referred to as Atma, Buddhi and Manas with the qualities of these levels of being relating respectively to divine persistent will, love-wisdom and abstract thought. The Soul is the repository of the essences of spiritual experience gained from all of our lives on Earth. We operate as the Soul's instrument in the lower worlds of creation and contribute towards its development by expressing these qualities whilst in incarnation.

Returning to the 'leaves on a tree' analogy offered by Annie Besant, the human personality utilises the environment into which it is thrust for the purpose of expressing the qualities of the Soul which are then stored at the level of the Higher Self. These hard-won spiritual attributes contribute to the development and growth of the Soul, in terms of unfolding its symbolic petals, whilst also being available to the personality in subsequent incarnations.

We are therefore required to express the quality of Atma, or divine persistent will, in our spiritual endeavours both in terms of symbolically clinging to a narrow precipice on the mountain of initiation whilst all around us is crumbling, and in subjecting our personality vehicles to the disciplines of the path.

Similarly, we must develop and display the qualities of the buddhic plane of consciousness which are encapsulated by the phrase, 'Love Wisely Applied and Wisdom Lovingly Applied'.

We must also exercise the quality of Higher Manas or abstract thought. This relates to our ability to think of matters in life which are not related to our survival instincts or to the fulfilment of the various desires associated with our lower nature. Abstract thought is exercised by studying the arts, philosophy and, of course, the classical esoteric teachings. The development of abstract thought is greatly enhanced by studying and interpreting the symbolism of myth and the imagery associated with dreams and meditation.

As I have stated previously, abstract thought represents the current frontier in human consciousness. The lower mind or intellect is related to the four lower sub-planes of the plane of Manas or mind.[2] The three upper sub-planes relate to abstract thought or Higher Manas which is related to the archetypal realm of consciousness so effectively described by Jung, and which Plato described as the 'World of Ideas'.

The practice of abstract thought provides us with a means of understanding the energies of the archetypal realms and of developing the faculty of higher mind. In doing so we are able to extend our consciousness to levels beyond that of the intellect as a means of ascertaining and aligning ourselves to the archetypal energies which drive humanity forwards towards the realisation of its divine purpose. This is the means by which we construct the antakarana with the objective of connecting with the intent of the Soul whilst being infused by its energies and qualities.

Jung illustrated how the archetypal energies which underlie the patterns of life upon our planet, and which drive humanity forward towards the realisation of its purpose, are represented within the human psyche as symbols. In Chapters 12 to 15 we shall consider the instrumental role which the archetypes play in the realisation of the divine plan and the profound importance which an understanding of symbolism offers to us as we tread the path.

The Soul is formless yet it is often likened to a giant lotus in the process of opening its three tiers of petals relating to Knowledge, Love and Sacrifice. The classical teachings state that symbolically it requires 777 lives for the Soul to learn every lesson that life in human form has to offer. These teachings state that the first 700 of these lives relate primarily to the opening of the knowledge petals, the next 70 lives to the opening of the love petals and the last 7 lives relate to the opening of the sacrifice petals whereby one performs acts of great sacrifice towards the betterment of humanity and the planet where personal needs are cast aside as one dedicates one's life's endeavours towards these ends. The number of lives required for the Soul to fully develop and express its qualities of Atma, Buddhi and Manas can be reduced when we tread the path of return. By doing this we may compact the learning experiences and spiritual growth of many lives into a short few. As the symbolism relating to the ascent of the cliff-face of the mountain of initiation suggests, this is a difficult and most demanding process.

Mahayana Buddhism talks of Sukhavati—the realm of bliss. The wisdom teachings use the term Devachan in reference to the true heaven state where the Soul rests between incarnations and where the aspirations of the previous life are developed into faculty and the experiences of it converted into wisdom. Devachan is a state of spiritual consciousness which is commensurate with the spiritual content of the previous life.

Sukhavati is described as a lake containing many lotuses which represent the Souls of humanity. These lotuses are at varying stages in terms of the opening of their petals and their ultimate flowering. Some are fully opened displaying their beauty and emitting their fragrance whilst others are at the stage of budding. In the light of the classical teachings it may be stated that the flower of the Soul forms a bud in the case of a young Soul, an opening lotus with three tiers of petals in one who is treading the path, and a resplendent blossom containing a blazing, radiant Jewel in the Lotus in the spiritual initiate.

A thread of energy known as a sutratma connects the Soul to its personality. This enables the Soul to constantly impart meaning and direction to the personality engaged in physical incarnation. In our early incarnations the sutratma is but a tenuous thread. However, through the cumulative effective of continued incarnations, and particularly through spiritual practices, and especially that of meditation, the sutratma is widened and converted to a channel. This then forms the antakarana or rainbow bridge which eventually allows a dialogue to occur between the higher and lower selves. The Soul rewards the personality which aspires towards spiritual growth with deluges of spiritual energy passing down the antakarana. This energy floods into the aura and through the chakras, especially those of the head and the heart. In summary, the human constitution may be described as follows:

The Monad or divine spark—our spiritual essence;
The Soul or Higher Self—comprised of the qualities of Atma, Buddhi and Manas and;
The Personality—comprised of the physical, astral and mental bodies.

As human personalities we take on a new body and particular set of circumstances in each life. These are appropriate to our spiritual development. This process begins its new cycle when the Soul, in accordance with the will of the Planetary Logos (the greater being within which it resides) asserts its will-to-be. It extends part of itself down onto the mental plane where a structure appropriated by the Soul, known as the mental permanent unit, vibrates and attracts towards it mental atoms of a similar nature and a mental sheath is formed. This structure will develop into the mental body. The Soul then, from within the mental sheath, activates the astral permanent atom, the corresponding structure on the astral plane, and in the same way an astral sheath is formed which in turn will develop into an astral body. The sheaths hover over a fertilised human egg, pre-selected by the Soul. Progressively the embryo and foetus are occupied. As the child grows into an adult the Soul increases its hold on the physical body of which the constitution is determined by the structure of the physical permanent atom located at the level of the etheric plane. The ability of the Soul to harness the physical body to its intent is affected greatly by the extent of the spiritual orientation of the personality which the Soul has assumed.

The permanent atoms may be considered as the counterparts to our DNA. It is by virtue of these mechanisms that the monad can fulfil its objectives on planes of consciousness below its own. The permanent atoms which comprise the Soul are located at the levels of

Atma, Buddhi and Manas. Collectively these form the relatively permanent structure known as the Causal Body. This is the centre of Soul consciousness which endures throughout our many incarnations until it is dissipated at the fourth initiation. The permanent atoms of Atma, Buddhi and Manas effectively serve as a 'cosmic bank' whereby our expression of the spiritual qualities related to these planes is stored for subsequent use both in our current life and in those which follow. The content of the mental unit (a reflection of the permanent atom at the level of Manas), the astral permanent atom and the physico-etheric permanent atom, as shaped by our response to, and the use of the energies of these respective planes, determine the nature of the corresponding personality bodies of each incarnation.

The personality, to some extent, expresses the purpose of the Soul by virtue of expressing its qualities of Atma, Buddhi and Manas. Eventually, the personality discards its physical body at the end of the incarnation. At death, the Soul progressively vacates the physical and etheric bodies prior to residing within the astral world for a variable period of time. At the 'second death' when the astral body is discarded the spiritual qualities expressed in the last life are extracted and experienced as bliss at what Douglas Baker describes as the 'hub of the wheel' where the Soul rests between lives in the true-heaven state of Devachan located at the level of the mental plane. The Soul remains in Devachan until the will-to-be is again asserted and the cycle of rebirth is resumed.

There are numerous laws which determine the length of the period which one spends on the astro-mental and higher planes between lives. This is not of concern in relation to this work. It is appropriate to state here however, that young Souls who are as yet unable to adequately express the qualities of the Higher Self barely merit periods in Devachan and thus incarnate very quickly between lives. Advanced Souls often choose to renounce Devachan as a means of proceeding more rapidly with their development as they traverse the spiritual path.

CHAPTER 7

THE FACTOR OF KARMA

THE GREAT LAW OF KARMA WORKS CEASELESSLY, endeavouring to bring the universe and all of its inhabitants into a state of balance and harmony. By virtue of this, all aspects of creation may achieve their optimum potential and ultimately return to their divine source. Karma serves an educational purpose by returning the results of our actions to us for our personal experience, our consideration and our spiritual growth.

Karma ensures the complete development of the Soul in terms of its engagement and enmeshment with matter, together with its final liberation from the world of physical form thereby guaranteeing the construction of the Soul as a lotus. The factor of Karma drives us through our long series of incarnations through its Law of Cause and Effect. It is by means of this that we continue our experiences. Through knowledge of reincarnation and karma it is possible for us to perceive that the conditions of life which we find ourselves in at present can be understood as being the result of activities performed in our previous lives.

Probably the most famous quote in respect of karma is found within the Bible where St Paul states 'whatever a man soweth, that shall he also reap'.[1] The analogy of sowing and reaping is a particularly apt way of describing this great universal law. In esoteric astrology the planet Saturn rules the scythe and, together with the sign of Capricorn, also rules long-standing karma going back over many lives.

In his classic work, *The Jewel in the Lotus,* Douglas Baker outlines the immense nature of the subject of karma:

> '*The subject is immense. Not even a Master of the Wisdom can discourse with certainty on karma for He too, is subject to the karmic forces of immense Beings in Whom we all live and move and have our Being...The blood cells, the nerve cells and the muscle cells of our bodies are living things and are, therefore, subject to karma—even to the karma of the one in whom they live and move and have their being! A man, put under stress by an anti-social action, may flee the police. For weeks he might be on the run. The cells in his body must suffer the effects of raised blood pressure, of sudden 'epidemics' of toxic materials like carbon dioxide, lactic acid, etc., which stem from the excessive exertions of 'the one in whom they live ... ', as he eludes capture. Substitute any human for one of those cells and we soon get an idea of the vast implications and extent of the karma for humanity.*'[2]

What the classical teachings advise us of in relation to karma is that when we take our own evolution in hand we seek to become a more suitable instrument of divine expression. As a means of achieving this we are challenged to eradicate any negative or involutionary qualities whilst developing positive or evolutionary ones. The offloading of karma can greatly assist this process and should be viewed as a great spiritual opportunity regardless of any scenarios that we may find ourselves thrust into.

When we make the decision to consciously accelerate our spiritual development as we respond to the pull of the monad, or what Joseph

Campbell described as '*the call to adventure*', we must be prepared to shed karma at a very rapid rate. When such a decision is made the Soul then pays considerably more attention to its instrument of expression and will test the personality accordingly to determine its reliability as a spiritual mechanism. We must be aware that everything that confronts us in life is of our own doing, whether good or bad, but that this is always employed towards our spiritual development.

In relation to the factor of karma we must bear in mind that good, as well as bad karma has the same binding effect as we seek liberation from the Wheel of Rebirth. The payment of karmic debt is used by the Higher Self to develop each individual so that, in its payment, we may display courage, patience and endurance in the face of difficult or challenging karma. If the karmic dispensation is 'good' then the benefits that accrue to the individual should be given out for the benefit of others. During the course of his many lectures Douglas Baker stated on numerous occasions that the best way to rapidly relieve oneself of difficult karma is to perform acts of service to humanity and to the planet.

CHAPTER 8

AS ABOVE SO BELOW

IN THE LIGHT OF THE WISDOM TEACHINGS, IT HAS been demonstrated that the long evolutionary journey of the Soul, as the instrument of the monad, occurs within a living universe whereby all things found therein 'live within the body of a greater being'. As a means of further enhancing our understanding of the evolutionary process we must now have recourse to Postulate Three of the Ancient Wisdom which informs us that 'all things are made in the image of the one in whom they live and move and have their being'.

The famous Hermetic axiom, 'As Above, So Below' is commonly used to describe the correspondence between microcosm and the macrocosm ergo the solar system is a microcosm in relation to our universe whilst our planet Earth is microcosmic to the Sun. Humanity is microcosmic to the Earth.

The One Divine Life, which pervades our entire universe, displays similar qualities in the various forms and kingdoms of nature through which it activates and expresses itself. Every form lies within its own aura and is fed from within through subtle threads from higher dimensions via a sutratma. This energy emanates from that form's Soul or Higher Self. This statement holds true for a mineral, a plant, an animal, a human being, a planet, a solar system and so on.

The human form may be described as the Grand Archetype or the Grand Symbol of the Universe. The human form is the progenitor of all forms which, whilst being subject to the effects of their natural environment, are produced through the radiation of its archetypal energies which provide the blueprint for evolution to occur, both physical and spiritual. The human form supplies the impetus and energy for invisible hierarchies of life, the angelic beings or devas, to build lesser forms which forever strive towards emulating the grand archetype. This subject is beyond the scope of this work and the reader is referred here to H.P. Blavatsky's classic work, *The Secret Doctrine* and Douglas Baker's book, *Anthropogeny: The Esoteric History of Man's Origin*.

Of all the forms in the various kingdoms of nature, both visible and invisible, including the angelic, the human form provides the best balance between spiritual and material substance. It represents a wonderful fusion of spiritual qualities such as divine will, love, compassion, intuition, and abstract thought with gross substances such as iron, calcium, nitrogen, phosphorus and the various other components of the gross physical body.

There are less spiritual forms than the human which are grosser in nature, and there are more spiritual forms than the human without the density of physical substance. The human form represents the greatest balance between the spiritual and the material and exists for the purpose of spiritualising matter. Life cannot evolve to any great extent within a planetary system without a human presence whether this occurs at mental, astral, etheric or physical levels.

The human form is used to understand the universe which it mirrors whether one is seeking to comprehend the workings of macrocosmic structures (including the Planetary Logos and the Solar Logos) or microcosmic ones (such as atoms and molecules). Paracelsus, the great medieval alchemist stated that, *'Man is a solar system in miniature'*. The scientist, philosopher, theologian and mystic

Emmanuel Swedenborg used to say that 'the entire creation is only a titanic man, and we are made in the image of the Universe'. These statements uphold the correspondence between the greater, or macrocosm, and the lesser, or microcosm.

It is worth noting that every cell possesses a central nucleus that functions as its vital structure. The heart operates in a similar manner in the human form. Likewise the Sun represents the heart or nucleus of our solar system whilst our galaxy possesses a galactic centre.

In his autobiographical work, *Memories, Dreams, Reflections*, Carl Jung states that the human psyche is set up in accord with the structure of the universe, and that what happens in the macrocosm likewise happens in the infinitesimal and most subjective reaches of our psyche. Just as the monads operating through human forms are engaged upon a long evolutionary journey to develop and express their inherent spiritual qualities, so this process is occurring both throughout the lower kingdoms of nature and in the greater beings within which we, as members of humanity, reside. As we seek spiritual transformation so we contribute to the evolution of the planetary and solar beings of which we are a part who are undergoing the self-same process at a considerably higher level on the evolutionary scale.

As stated in Chapter 4, the process of yoga is taking place at human, planetary, solar levels and beyond. If we were to embark upon a study of the history of ideas these may be viewed in an entirely different perspective from orthodox opinion if they are considered as being inspired from the causal realms of the psyche and occurring within the context of Planetary Psychosynthesis, and all that this process entails.

In respect of the esoteric fact that the macrocosm transmits itself into each of its microcosms, Douglas Baker frequently utilised the analogy of the hologram to demonstrate this profound hermetic truth. On this subject he writes:

> *'This basic concept of the similitude of the parts to the whole and their intimate interconnection is beautifully represented in the modern development of the hologram. The hologram is a three-dimensional reproduction resulting from the interference pattern*

Adaption of Robert Fludd's 16th century woodcut of 'Vitruvian man' by Zachariel

produced by two coherent laser beams of light. One beam is reflected off the object to be holographed, and the other beam acts as the reference. The two laser beams meet on a photographic plate, together creating an interference pattern which produces the hologram. The unique feature is that each part of the hologram contains the image and information of the whole. In other words, each point on the hologram is a complete mirror image of the whole original object.

'One of the astounding effects of incorporating a holograph onto a plate is that not only will the plate reflect say, for instance, the image of the human brain, but if the plate is shattered, each splinter of it will reflect the same complete image of the brain.

'Analogously, each individual entity is created in the image of God and, therefore, is a blueprint in miniature of the entire Universe. This is true in two important respects. First of all, everything, no matter how large or how minute, is created in the image of the One Absolute Reality. And more particularly, each entity is created in the image of 'the one in whom it lives and moves and has its being.' Thus, for example, a blood cell is a mirror image

of the entire Universe, but at the same time it is more particularly an image of the entity (i.e. human) in whom it has its being.'[1]

We witness analogies in the lower kingdoms of nature, mineral, plant and animal, which represent the archetypal process of spiritual transformation. In doing so, in accordance with the principle of 'As Above So Below', we are offered insight into the conditions which we may expect to encounter as we seek to realise our spiritual potential as members of the human kingdom. As an example, the production of diamonds in the mantle of the Earth under particular conditions of intense pressure and high temperature provides an analogy of the alchemical process whereby one undertakes the necessary practice and discipline towards rendering oneself a worthy recipient of the fiery spiritual energies associated with the process of spiritual initiation. The formation of diamonds occurs at considerable depth within the lithospheric mantle; similarly, the transformation of the human personality into an effective instrument of the Soul is a most challenging and subjective event which occurs at deeply concealed levels of the human psyche.

Continuing with our consideration of the analogies of the process of spiritual transformation in the lower kingdoms of nature, the embryonic growth and development of the flowering plant is probably the most perfect illustration of this process. If we were to use a microscope to observe the tip of a rose bud then we would witness that the cells found there are undergoing immense stress and strain due to the effort required for the plant to flower. Similarly, as we tread the spiritual path we undergo the self-same process as we seek to give expression to the qualities of the Soul. It is very challenging for us to renounce various material and social aspects of our life which have previously served us well. Unlike our endeavours of the past which have produced clear and tangible results, and often the approval and admiration of others, we are now challenged towards establishing a bridgehead into the higher worlds for the purpose of unfolding the symbolic lotus petals of the Soul. As personalities, there will be instances where we must let the Soul do its work in fashioning us into an effective spiritual instrument. We must endure the pressure and the associated pain of this process together with the alternations between light and darkness, joy and suffering.

Eventually, the flower blooms in full and its ultimate perfection is achieved. We, too, eventually flower into a perfected being expressing the qualities of the Soul which Plato described as truth, beauty and goodness with these being radiated outwards to the world.

The Soul is commonly symbolised as a lotus-like structure. The lotus has its roots in the earth representing our physical body or earthly base. Its stem grows in water symbolising the astral or emotional level of our being. The lotus flower opens above, in the air, which represents the level of the mind and its central role in the process of our spiritual development. The flowering of the lotus occurs through its exposure to the rays of the Sun symbolising our spiritual essence—the monad. The fact that the lotus flowers above the water suggests that we must develop the capacity to operate at a level above or beyond that of the emotions thereby avoiding kama-manas. It is desire which binds us to the Wheel of Rebirth and to the maya of the lower worlds which Madame Blavatsky described as a 'magic-lantern show'. Desire arises through our identification with, and our attachment to, the transient objects and circumstances of the material world. We cannot express the immortal, enduring part of our being if our efforts in life are based upon, and driven by, the pursuit of matters of an impermanent nature. This is a very important consideration as we tread the path. We must seek liberation from the hegemony of the astral body and its associated desires.

There are four main desires which underlie human activity and which bind us to the Wheel of Rebirth:

1. *The Desire for Recognition* (related to the astrological element of fire and the signs—Aries, Leo and Sagittarius)
2. *The Desire for Security* (related to the astrological element of earth and the signs—Taurus, Virgo and Capricorn)
3. *The Desire for New Experience* (related to the astrological element of air and the signs—Gemini, Libra and Aquarius)
4. *The Desire for Response* (related to the astrological element of water and the signs—Cancer, Scorpio and Pisces)

It is important for us to be aware that desire is healthy, in the early stages of human evolution, as the monad seeks to engage with and experience matter. Such desire serves to immerse the Soul in material existence whereby it can experience all that life in physical form has to offer. However, at a certain stage of our evolution when we experience divine unrest, and begin to tread the path, we are challenged not to function in a puppet-like manner driven by the strings of our various desires, rather, we must transmute desire into spiritual aspiration as we seek to access and express the energies and the intent of the Soul.

CHAPTER 9

ALL LIFE IS INTERCONNECTED

W E HAVE ALREADY ESTABLISHED THAT ONE LIFE pervades all forms within our universe and that these forms serve as vehicles for aspects of the One Divine Life, the monads, to develop and express spiritual qualities. It is therefore logical for us to arrive at the conclusion that all life is interconnected within a vast continuum. Postulate Four of the Ancient Wisdom advises us here that, 'there is a continuum which links all living things together so that the smallest cell does not pulsate without its effects being felt in the furthest reaches of the solar system'.

The ceaselessly changing motion of the planets of our solar system set against the backdrop of the surrounding zodiacal constellations indicates both the conditions inherent within the universal physiology and those of the human psyche in a dynamic, interactive and mutually influential process. This occurs through the agency of the universal continuum. The effects here are exerted upon not just humanity, but indeed all kingdoms of nature with these interacting in various ways as components of the greater beings within which they reside.

As members of humanity we are part of a greater being whose chakras are constituted by the various Root Races. Humanity exists within its own particular continuum. The experiences of each member of humanity exert their effects upon the other members of our particular kingdom of nature. This occurs both in terms of present conditions and in the formation of future patterns of expression, whilst also being influenced by the past experiences of members of the human kingdom.[1]

As members of humanity we exert great pressure upon our environment through the continuum which links all life. The first postulate informed us that 'all things live', including our thoughts which exist and radiate their expression in the mental, astral and etheric realms, even if these do not reach physical expression. It is apparent, therefore, that our thoughts of a negative nature, including those which are anxious, attaching or harmful, serve to exert detrimental effects both upon ourselves and others. However, the reverse of the metaphorical coin here is that through generating positive thoughts we may then become a powerful force for good by stimulating the evolution of humanity and the planet in general. This provides substance to the practices of our various world religions which affirm certain principles of behaviour relating to thought, word and deed.

The emphasis of this postulate is that energy is transmitted in realms of matter and levels of consciousness considerably more subtle than that which contemporary science can adequately measure and assess. As we have seen, the seven planes of existence range from the logoic to the physical. Each of these planes is divided into seven sub-planes. The material of these sub-planes becomes rarer and more electro-magnetic as one proceeds upwards from the seventh, or lowest, to the first or highest. The material of the highest sub-plane on each level is comprised of anu, or ultimate atoms which are in fact energy vortices. They provide the energy and the medium through which much of the phenomena of the continuum occur serving to receive, transmit and transmute the energy from higher to lower planes.

The anu were clairvoyantly observed by the eminent Theosophists C.W. Leadbeater and Annie Besant as they investigated the structure of chemical elements and compounds as a means of observing their fundamental constituents. Their work here began in 1895 continuing until 1933. A significant number of their findings were published in their work entitled *Occult Chemistry* in 1908. Besant and Leadbeater were observing, at that time, what today is described as quantum states of matter.

The field of Quantum Physics is now beginning to offer evidence of our dynamic, interactive and interconnected universe. The quantum is a unit of energy found at sub-microscopic dimensions which form the microscopic realms of existence. Its discovery is indicative of the fact that science is now aware of the existence of substance more subtle than that previously known, and that there is still considerably more to be found and understood in this respect. Science has named these unknown areas 'dark energy' and 'dark matter'. It is likely that the quantum levels of existence recently discovered, correlate to the etheric sub-plane with dark matter relating to astral matter and dark energy being connected with mental substance.

The discoveries of quantum physics have revolutionised the views of science in terms of our relationship to the material world. The Danish physicist Neils Bohr made foundational contributions to quantum theory. Bohr was aware that the outer material world does not function independently, but rather that it is inextricably linked to the manner by which we perceive it. When we observe a microscopic (quantum) system, we change it. This can be attributed to the factor of consciousness by virtue of the effects that we create upon the mental and astral planes and which impinge upon the etherico-physical level. In simple terms the observer cannot be separated from that which he is observing and that every physical process contains both objective and subjective features.

On this matter, my friend and co-worker within the Claregate Group, Paul Wright, states:

'Our ability to observe and to participate in that which we observe, demands a radical shake-up in our view of the true nature of

Reality. Our ability and power to adapt will be tested through and through as we face the weird, unpredictable and uncertain nature of quantum laws and their dynamics. We will come to realise how we affect that which we observe and how, what we observe, in turn affects us. We will find out that our macrocosmic and our microcosmic dimensions respond to the same underlying laws and are far from separate, despite the fact that classical science stubbornly upholds that the laws that govern them respectively are different, but this stubbornness is indeed short lived as physicists come to realise that the enigmatic nature of the quantum worlds that raises so many questions can only be resolved through the inclusion of Consciousness as an integral part of their research.'[2]

The relationship between the observer and the observed bestows a great duty upon humanity. This factor suggests that humanity possesses an important role in the universe as a participator in terms of observing the various kingdoms of nature thereby creating affects within these whilst they, in turn, simultaneously affect humanity. As was demonstrated in the previous chapter, the human form represents the grand archetype from which all other forms are derived. Life within a planetary scheme cannot evolve to any great extent in the absence of a human presence.

When we consider the relationship between the observer and the observed in the light of Postulate Two, i.e., 'all things live within the body of a greater being', it suggests that Sanat Kumara—the Lord of the World[3], also known as the Silent Watcher, is in the participator role in terms of our planet and that his observations exert their effects upon humanity and the other kingdoms of nature, whilst that which he is observing simultaneously affects him. This concept can be extended to include the role of the Solar Logos, The One About Whom Naught May Be Said and indeed the transcendent and immanent factor within our entire universe which the Hindus describe as Brahman, as observers within their particular spheres of being.

CHAPTER 10

THE SEVEN RAYS

W E HAVE CONSIDERED THE LIVING DYNAMIC interconnected nature of our universe together with the role which we, as members of humanity, serve towards fulfilling its underlying intent. As a means of enhancing our understanding of the dynamics of our universe together with our capacity to align ourself to its evolutionary intent, it is now appropriate to introduce postulate five of the Ancient Wisdom. This states that 'our universe is constructed out of energies which resonate to seven qualities.'

The energies of the Seven Rays underlie the functioning of our entire universe. They are the great universal builders which are instrumental in the activation, construction and maintenance of our universe. The energies of the Seven Rays interact at every conceivable frequency upon the various planes of creation giving rise to planets, solar systems, galaxies, and so on. Everything within creation is subjected to the influence of the Rays.

The Seven Rays are derived from the AUM when the transcendent being, which the Hindus refer to as Brahman, sounds the note of universal creation with a vast outbreath. This emanates from the highest level of the seven Cosmic Planes of which the seven planes ranging from the logoic to the physical constitute but the lowest or cosmic physical plane of this vast evolutionary scheme.

The sounding of the AUM gives rise to the first three Major Rays of Aspect. These are Ray One of Will and Power, Ray Two of Love-Wisdom and Ray Three of Active Intelligence. The three Major Rays of Aspect are the fundamental or primary divine aspects which give rise to creation and underlie all Trinitarian religious teachings. Included here are the gods of the Hindu Trimurti.[1] Ray One of Will and Power corresponds with Shiva the god of destruction and transformation; Ray Two of Love-Wisdom corresponds with Vishnu the god of preservation and sustenance; Ray Three of Active Intelligence corresponds with the creator god Brahma. The three Major Rays of Aspect form the basis of the four minor rays, known as the Rays of Attribute. Each of Rays Four, Five, Six and Seven is therefore a combination of two or more of the major rays of aspect.[2]

The Seven Rays are filtered through the seven stars of Ursa Major—the Great Bear. This constellation is the outer manifestation of the seven head centres of The One About Whom Naught May Be Said. The Rays are then received into our Solar system through the Central Spiritual Sun. Thereafter, they flow from the Heart of the Sun outwards to the planets where they intermingle and blend with each other before reaching humanity.[3]

The Second Ray of Love-Wisdom is the Mother Ray of our solar system which, as we have seen, forms the heart chakra of The One About Whom Naught May Be Said. The dominant note or prevailing Ray energy within our Solar System, and the key to spiritual development is therefore that of Love-Wisely Applied and Wisdom-Lovingly Applied. The other six Rays are subsidiary to the Second Ray within the evolutionary scheme that is our solar system.

Gemini is the astrological sign most closely related to the Second Ray. This zodiacal sign rules duality and when we tread the path we are challenged towards unifying our dual nature of Soul and

THE SEVEN RAYS CORRESPONDENCES

* Average Man
** Man on the Path

RAY	1	2	3	4	5	6	7
QUALITY	Will and Power	Love-Wisdom	Active Intelligence	Art and Harmony	Concrete Knowledge	Devotion and Idealism	Ceremonial, Order, Ritual
COLOUR	Scarlet White	Indigo	Green	Yellow	Orange	Blue Rose	Violet
ZODIACAL SIGN	Aries, Leo Capricorn	Gemini, Leo, Virgo, Pisces	Libra, Cancer Capricorn	Taurus, Scorpio, Sagittarius	Aquarius, Leo, Capricorn Sagittarius	Virgo, Pisces Sagittarius	Cancer, Aries Aquarius Capricorn
PLANET	*Sun **Uranus	*Jupiter **Neptune	*Earth **Saturn	*Mercury **Mercury	*Venus **Venus	*Mars **Jupiter	*Moon **Eath
FOOD	Protein	Fats	Carbohydrate	Unknown	Vitamins	Water	Mineral Salts
MUSICAL NOTE	DOH	SOH	FAH	ME	RE	TE	LA
POLITICS	Fascism	Democracy	Socialism	City State	Oligarchy	Theocratic Despotism	Communism
GAS	Nitrogen	Oxygen	Hydrogen	Carbon Dioxide	Ammonia	Incense Laden	Nitrous Oxide
SENSE	Sight	Intuition	Hearing	Taste	Concrete Touch	Pain	Smell
PLANE	Adi Atmic	Logoic	Mental	Buddhic	Manasic	Astral	Etherico-Physical
NERVOUS Equipment	Cerebrum	Mid-Brain	Medulla	Cerebellum	Peripheral	Sympathetic	Para-sympathetic
Endocrine GLAND	Pineal	Thymus	Thyroid	Adrenals	Pituitary	Pancreas	Gonads
NATION'S SOUL	India China	UK USA	Unknown	Germany Austria	France	Italy Spain	Russia
NATION'S Personality	UK Germany	Brazil	China France	India Italy	Austria	USA Russia	Spain
SHAPE	Circle	Triangle	Square	Circle Squared	Sphere (lens)	Cube	Pyramid
CHAKRA	Head	Heart	Throat	Base of Spine	brow	Solar Plexus	Sacral
KINGDOM	Shamballa	Hierarchy	Deva	Humanity	Animal	Plant	Mineral

The Seven Rays: Table of Correspondences

personality. This is particularly emphasised when Gemini is placed on the Ascendant of the natal chart. However, the challenges and the rewards associated with this astrological archetype are applicable to us all as we journey towards the source of our being. The sign of Gemini, its planetary ruler Venus, and the 3rd house of the natal chart provide us with the capacity to create unity from duality whereby the intense conflict between Soul and personality is resolved in syzygy whereby the opposites are conjoined giving rise to what Jung described as Wholeness or Individuation. The challenge here is beautifully symbolised in the *Bhagavad Gita* where Arjuna is placed between the opposing armies of the Pandavas, representing the Soul and its attributes, and the Kauravas, symbolising our instinctual and desire-driven tendencies, on the battlefield of Kurukshetra.

The Rays manifest in cycles according to the evolutionary plan for our planet. Through their influence they produce the successions of civilisations and cultures which rise and then recede upon the Earth. At present the Sixth Ray which governed the Age of Pisces is passing out of manifestation whilst the Seventh Ray governing the Age of Aquarius rapidly coming in. We therefore witness a decline in devotional forms of religious worship and in the number of our monasteries whilst there is mounting concern for our over-polluted environment. We may also expect an increase in the use of various ritual practices in spiritual matters as this is a Seventh Ray quality.

Alice Bailey advised us of a New Renaissance which is due to commence around 2025 through the manifestation of the Fourth Ray of Art and Harmony through Conflict. The great civilisation of Ancient Egypt was governed by this Ray. We need only witness the great pyramids, the Sphinx, the temples of Luxor and Karnak and the artefacts of the tomb of Tutankhamun as a means of viewing wonderful illustrations of the effects of the Fourth Ray. The Ancient Greek civilisation, and its glorious culture, was ruled by the Fourth Ray as was the Mediaeval Renaissance which also contained strong elements of the Seventh Ray of Ceremonial Order and Ritual depicting the religious mysticism of the Catholic Church.[4]

The teachings related to The Seven Rays provide us with a contemporary key to the mysteries. Various methods towards treading the spiritual path have been developed throughout the ages and these should be appropriate to the language and qualities of the particular period in time. Previous keys to the mysteries here include those of sacred geometry, numerology, alchemy, esoteric anatomy and the Qabalah, to name but a few.

Esoteric Psychology represents a paradigm, or framework, for understanding all of life's processes whilst also providing us with the ability to utilise the hidden forces of nature whereby we may reconstruct the components of our psyche as a means of expressing the purpose of the Soul. The Table of Correspondences on page 67 illustrates the all-embracing nature of the Rays as the seven 'ultimate archetypes' which not only give rise to our universe, but whose evolutionary energies underlie all aspects of creation.

We shall now consider the Rays in respect of the esoteric human constitution. Our spiritual essence, the monad, is unchangingly located on one of the three Major Rays of Will and Power, Love-Wisdom or Active Intelligence. Approximately five per cent of human monads are found on Ray One, with the remaining ninety five per cent of monads distributed equally between Rays Two and Three.

The ray of the monad only becomes apparent at the advanced stage of human evolution referred to by the wisdom teachings as the 'third initiation' whereby the personality has been transfigured into a spiritual instrument and is able to work in accordance with the divine plan. It is after this particular initiation that the monad is definitely guiding the Soul.

The Soul, or Higher Self, is also governed by a particular ray. In the West, approximately two thirds of people have a Soul on the Second Ray of Love-Wisdom. The Ray of the Soul remains the same for around 28 lives. It is important to bear in mind here that the Soul, as the instrument of the monad, is seeking to extract the essence of every lesson that life in human form has to offer and therefore it will spend periods on each of the Seven Rays as a means of achieving this. During the course of treading the path the Ray of the Soul changes to one of the three Major Rays.

The personality also has its own Ray as does its constituent parts — the mental, astral and the physical. These generally change from life to life as the Soul seeks diverse forms of experience whilst simultaneously endeavouring to develop and express its qualities.

When we are aware of the various Rays that govern and influence our Soul, our personality and its mental, astral and physical bodies, we are offered deep and extremely valuable insights into the dynamics of our psyche. Esoteric Psychology provides us with knowledge of how to utilise the energy of the Soul. We become aware of our Soul's purpose in accordance with its particular Ray and we may then orientate our life towards these ends. We also understand how our personality and its mental, astral and physical bodies may be best utilised towards expressing the purpose of our Soul. We gain understanding of the workings of these vehicles of consciousness and of their responses as they are subjected to spiritual disciplines.

Whilst this chapter represents only a most brief introduction to the Seven Rays, the value of Esoteric Psychology becomes apparent to those who tread the path. Knowledge of our Ray Complement provides us with deep insight into our psychological predispositions, our strengths and limitations, as we seek to render ourselves as an effective instrument of the Soul. To gain further insight here you may wish to consult the following works: *Esoteric Psychology One* and *Two* and *Discipleship in the New Age One* and *Two* by Alice Bailey; *Esoteric Psychology: The Seven Rays* by Dr Douglas Baker; and *Tapestry of the Gods Volumes One* and *Two* by Dr Michael Robbins.

CHAPTER 11

MAYA: THE VEIL OF THE GODDESS

W E SHALL NOW CONSIDER POSTULATE SIX OF the Ancient Wisdom which teaches us that, 'the solidity and tangibility of the material world is an illusion. It is part of *maya*. All is energy manifesting as Fire and Form. Energy and matter are interchangeable.' The concept of maya is an abstruse one. Nevertheless, it is absolutely fundamental towards any serious advance in our spiritual development. In this respect, Douglas Baker observed:

> '*The Wisdom of the Ages has always said that all is energy and vibration. When energy manifests as matter, it produces illusion or maya. Matter is a very temporary focal point for energy, and that goes for all forms. But underlying all forms there is an energy pattern at a higher level constantly pulling matter into it. This is the real, enduring nature of a phenomenon—that which we call the noumen.*'[1]

He continues:

> *'Within us is a noumenal form or soul that works through a phenomenal body which has no real existence at all. It is an emptiness and nothingness without the energy transformer of the overshadowing soul… and we love that body and the material world in which it thrives…the material world that enmeshes us… ensnares us…surrounds us with a veil of glamour and diverts our attention from our real being.'*[2]

When we tread the spiritual path we seek to access and express the qualities and the intent of the immortal, enduring aspect of our nature amidst the realms of the transient. As we have seen, the purpose of the descent of spirit into matter is so that the monad may acquire *spiritual staying power*, this relating to our ability towards radiating and expressing our spirituality despite the many challenges which incarnation in matter presents.

The word maya is related etymologically to the word 'measure'. It is derived from the Sanskrit root 'ma'. We may view maya therefore as the measuring out of creation whereby the various forms found therein are displayed as an illusion. Essentially, maya causes the underlying One Divine Life to appear as many separate and distinct lives whilst rendering the transient, phenomenal world as real and enduring.

Indian teachings use the term 'shakti' to denote the active power of deity manifest. This is depicted symbolically in myth as the deity's goddess or consort. In India the symbolism of the lingam, or phallus, penetrating the yoni, or vagina, represents the transcendent being pouring out the energy of life into the field, or womb, of creation which is symbolised by the various goddess figures found in world mythology. When we contemplate the symbolism of the god and goddess in embrace we are pondering over the means by which life is generated together with its profound mystery. The active and passive powers of a single transcendent principle, which are essentially as one, appear as a duality.

On this subject the 20th century German Indologist Heinrich Zimmer writes:

Hylas and the Nymphs by John William Waterhouse

'There are many ways of representing the differentiation of the Absolute into antagonistic yet co-operative pairs of opposites. Among the oldest and most usual of these is that based on the duality of the sexes; Father Heaven and Mother Earth, Uranos and Gaia, Zeus and Hera, the Chinese Yang and Yin. This is a convention that has been developed with particular emphasis in the Hindu and later Buddhist traditions, where, though the outward symbolization in images is strikingly erotic, the connotations of all the forms are almost exclusively allegorical.'[3]

Joseph Campbell referred to the Goddess religions of India:

'She is time and space itself, and the mystery beyond her is beyond all pairs of opposites... everything is within her, so that the gods are her children.[4]

'The Indian name for that Being of all beings is brahman, which is a neuter noun, neither male nor female. And the Indian name for the woman is Maya-Shakti-Devi. "Goddess Giver of Life and Mother of Forms" ... It's the female as the giver of

forms. She is the one who gave life to the forms and she knows where they came from. It is from that which is beyond male and female. It is that which is beyond being and nonbeing. It is both and is not. It neither is nor is not. It is beyond all categories of thought and the mind.'[5]

Campbell would frequently state that the goddess symbolises 'all that can be known'. The secrets of the goddess, to which she holds the keys, are those of life itself. These are available only to those able to transcend her powers of maya. When we seek to perceive the spiritual symbolism found in world myth, it is most helpful to regard goddess figures as symbols of the energies and processes inherent in the various realms of creation and as the means by which deity is able to manifest. The goddess factor can be found in all levels of existence beneath the first cause. It is therefore, within the realm of the goddess that we, as monads, undertake our long evolutionary journey in pursuit of acquiring spiritual staying power.

When creation manifests, duality occurs: the One becomes two. All that is found within nature contains pairs of opposites: spirit and matter; male and female; subjective and objective; light and dark; positive and negative polarities; good and evil and so on. Opposites enable us to distinguish one object from another, one state of being from another by means of comparison. They stand each to the other as points of reference. It is through experiencing such opposites that the Soul learns truth—to discriminate between Self and not-Self, reality and unreality, and ultimately to attain the state of unity which both underlies and transcends the duality of manifestation.

The great 8th century Hindu philosopher Shankara elaborated upon ideas found within the *Upanishads* and these, together with his commentaries on the *Brahma Sutras* and the *Bhagavad Gita*, served to establish the teachings of Advaita Vedanta. The reasoning of this great Indian sage was based upon the Vedic formula or Mahavakya (meaning 'great saying') of the *Chandogya Upanishad—Tat Tvam Asi*[6] or 'Thou Art That'. Shankara regarded the Self or Atman (the monad) as the only reality. He described how the attributes of the ego or personality are mistaken for the Self, and of how maya teases our perception whilst the Self remains deeply concealed. However, when the Self is 'known' then maya ceases to exist.

Shankara gave a famous illustration of maya. When walking down a dark road the sight of a coiled rope is mistaken for a snake. Upon closer inspection the truth is revealed and the illusion one experiences here is then shattered. When the rope is known, the snake vanishes. Similarly, when we are able to *realise* that creation is infused by the one divine life, described by the Vedanta teachings as Brahman, then the world of multiplicity vanishes.

The concept of maya does not relate to the fact that what we see or experience has no existence. It means rather, that we are blinded, and our minds distorted by our own imperfections. These prevent us from apprehending the *real* or inner nature of that which we perceive. We are therefore unable to arrive at a true interpretation of the world that surrounds us. The world of appearances blinds us in terms of recognising the One Divine Life which is inherent within all forms. The imperfect mind is unable to perceive perfect truth so instead it toils under an illusion in accordance with its own imperfections — a maya.

In modern society maya takes the form of materialism and related matters which invoke and excite our desire nature, of which it is our purpose to transmute into higher spiritual qualities if we are to succeed in treading the path. We must bear in mind that the Soul chooses the circumstances of each incarnation and selects those most suitable towards furthering its development and growth. When the advanced Soul chooses to incarnate into a contemporary culture it is seeking to test the personality in terms of its ability to develop and express its qualities amidst the many challenges which life within such an environment presents. If we can succeed in this respect then it represents a great leap forward in the development and growth of the Higher Self.

When we seek spiritual transformation we are challenged to *realise* that the manifest world consists of what the Vedanta teachings refer to as 'names and forms' derived from the divine sound, the AUM, and which are therefore part of the 'dream of Brahman'. We must be aware that we are located at the midpoint of two opposite poles (pure spirit and dense matter) and that our attention should be firmly focussed on the objectives of the former.

As a means of achieving such a realisation we must undertake the disciplines of the path. The successful practice of these can enable us to not only understand intellectually how maya operates, but to function as an instrument of the Soul in our daily lives, the immortal being that resides at a level of consciousness beyond the manifest opposites of the lower worlds.

In Jungian terms this is achieved by one attaining individuation. On this matter Frieda Fordham states:

'The individuation process is sometimes described as a psychological journey…a truer description would be that of a spiral. In this journey the traveller must first meet his shadow…There is no wholeness without recognition of the opposites. He will meet, too, with the archetypes of the collective unconscious, and face the danger of succumbing to their peculiar fascination. If he is fortunate he will in the end find the treasure hard to attain, the diamond body, the Golden Flower, the lapis, or whatever name or guise has been chosen to designate the archetype of wholeness, the Self.'[7]

When we experience the the pull of the monad the path of return beckons. We are challenged towards disengaging our consciousness from the attractions of the lower worlds, to become oblivious to the enticements of maya. At this stage of our long evolutionary sojourn, desire, which has served its purpose in enabling the monad to engage fully in the affairs of the external world, must now be overcome.

We must relinquish our desire towards attaining status and achieving recognition in life. We must eradicate our need for emotional security whether this is obtained through the accumulation of wealth and possessions, through human relationships or by any other means. We should not be overwhelmed by sensual pleasures at the expense of our subjective development. We must also extricate ourselves from the demands of society and any perceived duties here. The classical teachings inform us as to the futility of such pursuits for the individual treading the path as these are aspects of maya. Such forms of desire must be transmuted into aspiration for that which is transcendent and eternal.

In his best known work, *The Republic*, Plato famously depicted maya in his cave allegory. He asked his students to visualise a group of individuals facing a wall in a cave whereby they are shackled in such a manner that they can do nothing else but stare at the wall facing them. Behind them people are going about their daily business with the assistance of a lit fire which enables them to see what they are doing. Plato is comparing the world of the human personality, whereby one observes merely shadows on a wall, with the causal realms of the Soul where the genuine or real activity occurs and which gives rise to the silhouettes. Plato then asked his students to imagine what would happen if one of the prisoners could remove their shackles and turn around. As they observed the world behind it would come as a major surprise to them as they witnessed the activity which was causing the shadows to appear on the wall.

Pursuing the analogy further he then asked his students what the effect would be if one were taken out of the cave into the daylight, symbolising the light of their spiritual essence—the monad. This level of consciousness is related to the true source of the divine ideas which Jung described as 'archetypes'. After their eyes had adjusted to the power of the sunlight they would then possess a much clearer, and radically different, idea of the whys and wherefores of existence. This of course, represents one attaining a very high state of consciousness which the Hindus refer to as Samadhi and which here in the West we often refer to as the Superconscious Experience.

The light which one experiences here may also be taken to symbolise the higher initiations. We are then made aware of the purpose of existence, or we may say of the divine plan, as we are then cognisant of the intent of the one in whom we live and move and have our being. Thereafter we are required to convey the light of our experience to the rest of humanity as an act of service. Of course, like any great initiate one would encounter many difficulties and obstacles upon returning to the cave and trying to explain such an experience to one's fellow prisoners who steadfastly believe that reality consists of only shadows cast upon a wall.

CHAPTER 12

ARCHETYPES AND THE
COLLECTIVE UNCONSCIOUS

ARL JUNG REFERRED TO ARCHETYPES AS 'DIVINE
ideas' which govern and conduct the process of evolution.
He said that they are vast reservoirs of psychic energy
which form part of the collective unconscious. He portrayed the
collective unconscious as a boundless treasure house filled with
eternal images.

As we have seen, we are part of a living, dynamic and
interconnected universe. We reside within the environment of the
collective unconscious whose energy patterns not only give rise to
our consciousness, but also affect our reactions to the environment
surrounding us. We are constantly fed by, respond and donate to its
energies which pour out of archetypes, or reservoirs, which are found
in the precincts of our planet at subjective levels of being. In
demonstrating the important role of the archetypes, in terms of the
human condition, Jung says:

'A man likes to believe that he is the master of his soul. But as long as he is unable to control his moods and emotions, or to be conscious of the myriad secret ways in which unconscious factors insinuate themselves into his arrangements and decisions, he is certainly not his own master. These unconscious factors owe their existence to the autonomy of the archetypes.'[1]

In this chapter I seek to relate Jung's concept of the archetypes and the collective unconscious to the wisdom teachings. It is my opinion that this can serve towards both clarifying and enhancing our current understanding of Jung's ground-breaking work whilst providing an opportunity for humanity to develop further insights and applications in this respect. The Jungian analyst Marie-Louise Von Franz says that Jung:

'... was a pioneer and remained fully aware that an enormous number of further questions remained unanswered and call for further investigation... his views form an 'open system' that does not close the door against possible new discoveries.'[2]

In Greek myth the unconscious was the realm of Hades, the god of the underworld. The Romans used the name Pluto to describe their counterpart deity to Hades. This name is particularly apt in illustrating the spiritual riches found within the realm where he holds dominion; the Greeks and Romans created images of Hades and Pluto holding an overflowing cornucopia as a means of symbolising this. Jung demonstrated that it was through the experience and utilization of the riches found within the realms of the unconscious that we are given the opportunity towards achieving what he described as Individuation, whereby the conscious and unconscious aspects of the human psyche, including the Soul, are unified.

In esoteric astrology Pisces, its planetary ruler Pluto, and the twelfth house of the natal chart govern the unconscious. When this astrological archetype is prominent in our natal chart we are both particularly attuned and susceptible to its energies. It is no surprise therefore, that Pisces embraces the duality of both the highest and the lowest in life ranging from the spiritual treasures of the unconscious, located in the spiritual realms which Roberto Assagioli labelled the Superconscious, to crime, the criminal underworld and indeed all of the energies associated with the lowest astral sub-planes or Lower Unconscious. When Pisces is placed on the Ascendant in the natal chart one is advised to be prepared to journey through the chthonic hell regions of one's psyche as a means of attaining one's paradise. Whilst this is especially applicable to the Piscean Ascendant, it is relevant to us all as we tread the path and are confronted by the energies of the lower unconscious which we must successfully negotiate in the process of spiritual transformation.

The archetypes permeate the human psyche and human experience on all levels of being, creating structure and inciting evolutionary growth.[3] In applying the Hermetic axiom of 'As Above So Below' we may consider the archetypes as the brain cells of the Solar Logos which channel his projected thoughts, or 'divine ideas,' which guide and direct our destiny. The archetypes described by Jung are derived from both the energies and the interactions of the Seven Rays, the seven great cosmic builders whose energies underlie the functioning of our universe which we considered in Chapter 10. The archetypes under discussion here relate to the response of the Solar Logos to the Ray energies which impact upon him, and whose body constitutes the heart chakra of The One About Whom Naught May Be Said.

In her work *Esoteric Astrology*, Alice Bailey describes how the signs of the zodiac are comprised of, and express, various combinations of Ray qualities and that each planet within our solar system is governed by a particular Ray. It is the ceaselessly changing range of permutations created by the motion of the planets, set against the backdrop of the zodiacal signs, which conditions and influences human behaviour in multifarious ways by playing an instrumental role in the channelling and the expression of archetypal energies. As we have seen, the astrological natal chart represents a map of the psyche. It indicates the archetypal factors, derived from the influences of the planets and signs, which are operative in our lives. The natal chart reveals both the purpose of the Soul and the various factors of our psyche which may help or hinder us as we seek to express this. As divine ideas, the archetypes issue from our spiritual essence, the

*Assembly of twenty gods, predominantly the Twelve Olympians,
as they receive Psyche. By Raphael*

monad, and are then first expressed on the planes of consciousness
where the Soul resides, those of Atma, Buddhi and Manas, and which
have been collectively described by Roberto Assagioli and thereafter
by Douglas Baker as the Superconscious (this is outlined in the
following chapter). The archetypes enter the human aura through the
chakras and in their pure form they are generally expressed through
the chakras located above the diaphragm. Our instincts and drives
emanate from the lower realms of the unconscious in astral and in
mental substance. These are expressed through the chakras below the
diaphragm.

Jungian teachings state that the collective unconscious consists of
the instincts of humanity together with their correlates—the archetypes.
As members of the human kingdom we each possess instincts whilst
we are also subject to particular archetypal patterns which fashion our
lives. We each possess a personal unconscious and we are all attuned
to the collective unconscious. It is important for us to be aware that
our personal unconscious is merely a fraction of the vast sea of living
Fire which constitutes creation. It is but the crest of a minute wave
on the surface of this immense cosmic sea.

There is a reciprocal relationship between the archetypes and our instincts. Whenever an archetype expresses itself by emitting its energy downwards, there is a corresponding instinctual response. Similarly, if an instinct is beginning to manifest itself it will call down the energies of its associated archetype. It may be stated here that the energy reservoirs or morphic fields related to humanity (which we shall consider shortly) have been created by the responses of its members throughout the ages to the direction of archetypal energies which seek to facilitate the evolutionary journey of spirit through matter.

Archetypes and instincts converge in human consciousness. The individual who treads the path is confronted by this battleground between the Higher Self and the personality in the form of the spiritualising forces of the archetypes versus the instincts and desires. This is symbolised in the *Bhagavad Gita* by the battlefield of Kurukshetra where the good and righteous Pandavas do battle with the self-serving Kauravas, these two parties symbolising the archetypes and the instincts and desires respectively.

Our ability to express the pure energies of the archetypes, is determined by the extent of our spiritual evolution. Jung states that the average individual is dominated by the various instincts, desires, habits, impulses, prejudices and indeed every conceivable form of complex. He considered these to function like the Olympian deities who wish to be appeased, served, feared and worshipped, not only by the individual concerned, but also by those in their vicinity.

Shakespeare wrote in *As You Like It*[4] that 'all the world's a stage and all the men and women merely players'. This oft-repeated quote is given a deeper perspective when we are aware that the human personality represents a new role for the immortal actor—the Soul—and cognisant of the archetypal scripts which we, as members of humanity, are enacting as part of an evolutionary design for our planet. On this matter Joseph Campbell writes:

> *'All over the world and at different times of human history, these archetypes, or elementary ideas,[5] have appeared in different costumes. The differences in the costumes are the results of environment and historical conditions.'*[6]

The archetypal scripts which influence humanity are related to an evolutionary plan within a greater context which is designed towards unfolding the spiritual qualities of every monad within our solar system. The solar being may then realise its potential as part of an evolutionary design of considerably greater magnitude relating to the intent of The One About Whom Naught May Be Said.

As divine ideas the archetypes play an essential role in the process of evolution by guiding and directing the destiny of all life both on our planet and within our solar system. The archetypes are instrumental here both in terms of involution where we, as monads, descend into matter and in our spiritual evolution as we are called back to the source of our being.

Upon attaining the third initiation (which equates with Individuation or Psychosynthesis) one then has conscious access to the archetypes and to their numinous energies. The vibratory note which they sound is thereby in accord with that of the Solar Logos as they consciously act as an outlet for particular archetypal energies which are designed to implement the evolutionary plan for our solar system.

It is important to be aware that there is an interactive aspect to the archetypal scripts which are constantly being enacted upon our world stage. As well as governing and conducting the processes of evolution, the archetypes have been elaborated throughout our planetary history. All of humanity's thoughts and feelings, our comprehensions, our struggles, experiences of happiness, joy, beauty, and indeed every range of experience and feeling within the gamut of the human condition, are deposited into these giant reservoirs which exist within the precincts of our planet. Similarly, this occurs within the lower kingdoms of nature and particularly that of the animal where these contributions return as instinctual forces.

The English author, lecturer and parapsychologist, Rupert Sheldrake, outlined this matter in his revolutionary concept of Morphic Resonance. He postulates that memory is inherent in nature and that the members of the various organisms on our planet inherit a collective memory belonging to, and previously generated, by their particular species.

Sheldrake illustrates how all self-organising systems are comprised of component parts which themselves function on a holistic basis. In Chapter 4 you were introduced to the second postulate of the Ancient Wisdom which states that 'all things live within the body of a greater being'. It was demonstrated here that atoms are constituted by sub-atomic particles, and that similarly atoms are aggregated to form molecules which in turn reside within cells that can either exist or their own accord or they may combine to create more complex structures up to and including the human form. Sheldrake advises us that Morphic Fields are operative in such structures whereby they determine the characteristic properties of each self-organising system whilst they also serve towards interconnecting and coordinating the functioning of its integral parts. Every species possesses its own morphic fields and within each organism of any particular species fields exist within fields.

The theory of morphic resonance, in accordance with postulate two, is related to the 'greater beings' within which the aforementioned structures reside. Sheldrake labels the fields responsible for the development and maintenance of the bodily forms of plants and animals as 'morphogenetic fields' whilst he illustrates that the behavioural and mental activity of animals is dependent upon behavioural and mental morphic fields. Similarly he states that we, as members of humanity, are dependent on social and cultural morphic fields which have been elaborated by our ancestors, and indeed ourselves, in our previous incarnations!

When we considered the esoteric human constitution in Chapter 6 it was illustrated that the structure of our personality vehicles—the physical, astral and mental bodies—is determined by the content of their corresponding permanent atoms. In similar fashion, the structure of any morphic field is determined by that which has occurred before. Sheldrake argues that both genetic factors and morphic fields are involved in the factor of heredity. This is, of course, in contradiction to the prevailing orthodox theories of contemporary evolutionary biology. The theory of morphic resonance affords a broader perspective in this area which enables the idea of the inheritance of acquired characteristics to be taken more seriously. Sheldrake suggests that, by virtue of morphic resonance, the behaviours which organisms of a particular species learn, or the forms which they develop, may be inherited by others even though they are not descended from the original organisms.

Morphic fields operate on a basis of probability in a similar manner to quantum fields. They impose order and structure upon the organisms or systems which are subject to their influence. A consideration of the esoteric principles outlined by postulate two of the Ancient Wisdom enables us to be aware that morphic resonance is relative not merely to humanity and the lesser kingdoms, but also to the 'greater beings' within which we reside.

Sheldrake advises us that when a new morphic field arises it becomes increasingly potent through its repetition. By virtue of such repetition its organizing patterns become increasingly probable. On this basis, as Sheldrake argues, nature is essentially habitual.

Sheldrake's concept of Morphic Resonance suggests that when we engage in a particular action, feeling or thought we are contributing to a morphic field which absorbs this energy. The energy reservoir of the related morphic field then begins to reciprocate by feeding its accumulated energies back to us. This occurs throughout our many lives on Earth. The energies which are emitted contribute towards the collective unconscious with each of us possessing our own particular share of this via the morphic fields related to our permanent atoms. Such matters are worth considering when we witness diverse forms of human behaviour and expression: we are observing the effects of both the subjective energies of the archetypes and of the Morphic Fields which those concerned are accessing and expressing as they respond to the impulse generated from within.

This is why many events in our lives are of an archetypal nature in that when they occur there is reciprocity between the actual incident and the morphic field which it is related to. Major events of our lives include our birth, death, our separation from our parents, marriage and perhaps subsequent divorce. These, and many others, represent examples of this process. We also witness the presence and the effects of morphic fields in any matters which involve the process of learning. Contemporary examples here include the act of learning to drive, to operate and programme computers etc. In these, and many other cases the inherent memory pattern contained with the relevant morphic field assists us towards our chosen ends.

Jung showed that the unconscious, and the archetypal energies contained therein, may be viewed as a museum of parts derived from the history of the human psyche. On this subject he states:

> '*Just as the human body represents a whole museum of organs, each with a long evolutionary history behind it, so we should expect to find that the mind is organized in a similar way. It can no more be a product without history than is the body in which it exists.*'[7]

When considering the archetypes and Sheldrake's concept of Morphic Resonance it is important not to lose sight of the fact that the universe within which we reside is constantly evolving. As we have seen, there is an on-going relationship between humanity and the archetypes as they assist us in our spiritual development and growth. As a result of this, both we and the archetypes evolve. When we tread the path, we are accessing archetypal energies which include the efforts of those who have gone before us. Similarly, as we tread the path and respond to the archetypes associated with this, we then donate energy towards them, increasing the potency of the associated archetypes and their related morphic fields.

In undertaking the journey to the source of our being we benefit humanity as a whole, both in the respect of enhancing the particular archetypes associated with this, and in the fact that we become more effective instruments of spiritual expression by becoming more receptive to the archetypes in their original or true form. This also assists the development and growth of the greater beings within which we reside—the Planetary Logos and the Solar Logos.

In Chapter 16 we shall consider the important role which is played by the Psychopomp, the aspect of the Soul which assists us in our spiritual endeavours as we tread the path. We may consider the psychopomp as the archetypal pattern or morphic field which has arisen through the endeavours, throughout the ages, of outstanding members of humanity to achieve liberation from the Wheel of Rebirth.

We are unable to observe the archetypes directly. However, we may feel their energies and also view their manifestations in the outer world. As an example here, we cannot directly view the archetype of love but we can certainly both feel and witness its manifestation. The only tangible evidence we may obtain in respect of the archetypes is when they project their symbols and their images into our consciousness. Jung demonstrated that archetypes are represented within the human psyche as symbols. It is through this process that we may obtain guidance and direction from within.

It may be stated, within the context of this chapter, that what Joseph Campbell describes as 'The Hero's Journey' represents the challenge towards expressing the archetypes in their pure form as they are originally expressed on the planes of consciousness where the Soul resides. In undertaking this course of action the hero is challenged not to succumb to the astro-mental effects of the collective unconscious where the morphic fields developed by humanity throughout the ages orchestrate the actions and responses of the vast majority of its members. We shall witness aspects of this archetypal struggle symbolised in myth in Chapter 23 in three of the Labours of Hercules where the archetypal hero overcomes the Nemean Lion, the Lernaen Hydra and Cerberus the Guardian of Hades.

CHAPTER 13

THE SUPERCONSCIOUS

A S A MEANS OF ELABORATING UPON JUNG'S concept of a collective unconscious, various exponents of the wisdom teachings, including Roberto Assagioli and Douglas Baker, postulated the existence of a Superconscious. This is related to the planes of Atma, Buddhi and Manas where the Soul resides and from which levels of consciousness, the archetypes, are first expressed. We may consider this as a specific upper region located within what Jung describes as the 'collective unconscious' and which contains our highest potential. The energies of this realm exert a transformative and regenerative effect upon the personality.

Assagioli introduced his egg diagram (reproduced on page 91) as a means of mapping the basic structure and the dynamics of the human psyche and the collective unconscious. The diagram represents an elaboration upon Jung's concept of the collective unconscious. In respect of the egg diagram Assagioli writes:

'It is, of course, a crude and elementary picture that can give only a structural, static, almost 'anatomical' representation of our inner constitution, whilst it leaves out its dynamic aspect, which is the most important and essential one. But here, as in every science, gradual steps must be taken and progressive approximations be made. When dealing with a reality so plastic and elusive as our psychological life, it is important not to lose sight of the main lines and of the fundamental differences, otherwise the multiplicity of details is liable to obscure the picture as a whole and to prevent our realizing the respective significance, purpose and value of its different parts.'[1]

It is worth noting that there are certain variations of the particular model which is illustrated. As we briefly consider its content, it is important to bear in mind the permeable nature of the egg and that its interrelated contents are active, dynamic, and in a state of constant flux. You will note that dotted lines divide the contents within the egg demonstrating that their relationship to each other can facilitate psychological osmosis. The shell of the egg is also comprised of dotted lines. This illustrates the interrelationship between the individual and the collective unconscious. As the previous chapter demonstrated, we exist within the environs of the unconscious whereby the forces contained therein constantly influence our lives whilst we also donate our energies to the unconscious in our responses to its energies.

Assagioli's egg diagram describes the various regions of the unconscious in numeric form. The Superconscious or Higher Unconscious components of the diagram are depicted by numbers 3 and 9. The superconscious region is described, by exponents of Psychosynthesis, as the sphere of transpersonal qualities such as aesthetic experience, higher states of consciousness, genuine intuition, heroism, altruistic love, compassion, creative inspiration including feelings and insights of an artistic, philosophical or scientific nature, and as the source of genius.

Our personal share of the Superconscious, relating to the Soul, its functions and its evolutionary development, including our spiritual expression in previous lives, is indicated by number 3. This is where the archetypal energies relevant to our present incarnation, and which can assist us in the process of Psychosynthesis, are located in their purest form. The collective aspect of the superconscious, containing the overall content of the planes of Atma, Buddhi and Manas and the archetypal energies found here, is depicted by number 9.

The Self, as described by Assagioli, is indicated by number 6. It is located partly within and also partly outside of the egg. We may equate this to the transcendent and immanent qualities of the monad and from whose level of being the energies of the archetypes originate. Its mechanism, the Soul, resides within the Superconscious whose energies underlie the middle and lower unconscious and their associated activities. This demonstrates the immanent nature of the monad, whilst the location of Assagioli's Self partly outside of the egg illustrates its transcendent qualities.

The human personality or conscious 'I', and the ordinary field of consciousness within which it operates are represented by numbers 5 and 4 respectively. It is within this region of the psyche that our various experiences in life are assimilated. These are found within the Middle Unconscious. Our personal and the collective aspects of this realm are depicted respectively by the areas numbered 2 and 8. The middle unconscious is formed of psychological elements similar to those of our waking consciousness with these being easily accessible to us.

Although the middle unconscious is not within the remit of our conscious awareness it serves to support our normal conscious functioning. Our ability to develop skills, our behaviours, attitudes and feelings are conditioned by these areas of the unconscious whose forces and energies provide the foundation of our conscious life. The functioning of the middle unconscious is instrumental in all fields of human development and is self-evident in this respect. Children learning to walk and talk, the acquisition of language skills, developing proficiency in various professions and roles in society which we adopt, are a few of the numerous examples of humanity accessing the related morphic fields which have been created here by the past efforts of fellow members of the human kingdom.

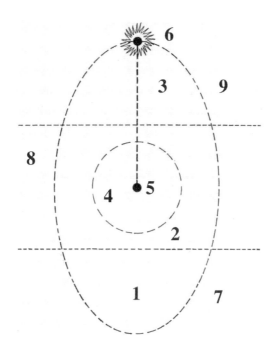

Roberto Assagioli's Egg Diagram to Map the Basic Structure and the Dynamics of the Human Psyche and Collective Unconscious

The Lower Unconscious is represented by numbers 1 and 7 which depict the personal and collective aspects of this realm respectively. The area related to number 1 includes our personal psychological past in the form of repressed complexes and long-forgotten memories. It is this realm of the psyche which contains experiences in our life related to fear, shame, anger, despair and other associated incidents which are consigned to this area beneath the surface level of our awareness. The energies related to our basic instinctual drives, so amply described by Freud, and necessary to the survival of primitive humanity, are found here.

The lower unconscious contains what Jung described as the 'Shadow', this being the part of ourselves which we refuse to acknowledge which is hidden, repressed, mainly inferior and guilt-laden. The shadow aspect of our psyche is commonly projected onto others. Jungian psychology advises us to both acknowledge and accept our shadow characteristics whereby we enter into a conscious and constructive relationship with the shadow as part of the individuation process. In conjunction with Jung's concept of the shadow, we find here the Dweller on the Threshold[2] as outlined by the wisdom teachings. The Dweller blocks the portal of initiation and is particularly adept at utilising the lower unconscious as a means of preventing our entry to higher states of consciousness.

When we undertake the evolutionary journey to the source of our being we seek to raise our consciousness so that we may access and express the energies of the realms of the Superconscious, and the archetypal energies found there, through the undertaking of spiritual disciplines, and particularly through meditation. Elements of the Superconscious may also precipitate into our consciousness in the form of intuitive thoughts and realisations, sudden forms of enlightenment and inspiration. By virtue of us undertaking spiritual disciplines the antakarana strengthens and widens. This establishes and enhances our relationship with the Soul and all that this process entails.

When we tread the path we must also confront and transmute that which is concealed within the Lower Unconscious. We are required to acknowledge and embrace our shadow characteristics and, as the wisdom teachings advise us prior to attaining the third initiation, to overcome the Dweller for the purpose of revealing what is referred to as the Angel of the Presence. This is the devic or angelic aspect of the Causal Body which guards the portal of initiation.

CHAPTER 14

ARCHETYPES AND THE PATH

JUNG DESCRIBED ARCHETYPES AS 'ORGANS OF THE Soul'. As we have seen, the archetypes are creative forces which profoundly influence the ways in which we think, feel and act. The energies which pour out of the archetypes shape our lives and actions and are the primary source of our ideas and creative inspiration.

When we tread the spiritual path we endeavour to express the archetypes which Plato described as Truth, Beauty and Goodness. These are related respectively to the three Major Rays of Aspect- Ray One: Will and Power; Ray Two: Love-Wisdom; and Ray Three: Active Intelligence. Towards these ends we are particularly concerned with our relationship to, and our expression of, the archetype of Wholeness. We seek here to invoke, or anchor to ourselves, something that will make us whole whereby we blend the psyche with the personality so that it will be complete. As we have seen earlier, this is the objective of Jung's individuation process whereby the conscious and unconscious aspects of the human psyche are unified. In achieving wholeness we are then able to function effectively in accordance with the intent of the Soul and therefore of the Planetary Logos, as the greater being within whom we reside.

The pursuit of Wholeness, or Psychosynthesis, is a matter which is existential in nature. Throughout our many lives we have been subject to all of the various combinations of the archetypal patterns related to the Seven Rays. Our unique reactions to their richly interwoven variety of conditioning energies, together with our responses to the energies of the ever-changing environments we have experienced, make us beings of completely individual and distinctive qualities. We therefore each possess our own particular requirements in consciousness. In Chapter 18 we shall consider certain aspects of the Grail legend as being representative of the spiritual quest. Here the knights embark upon their quest for the holy vessel with each of them entering the Forest Adventurous at their own chosen point. This illustrates that we must determine our own path by weaving the intent of our Soul upon the universal tapestry.

Whilst we must follow our own existential pathway in our spiritual endeavours the resultant goal of Psychosynthesis or Wholeness is common to us all. The astrological sign of Leo, its planetary ruler the Sun and the 5th house of the natal chart are closely associated with the archetype of wholeness. Leo rules royalty and therefore monarchs, crowns and thrones. When we embark upon the process of spiritual transformation we are challenged towards giving over sovereignty of our lives to the Soul. When this occurs, rather than operating in a self-centred and egotistical manner, allied to a pronounced sense of drama, we may function like a miniature Sun offering radiance, sustenance and illumination to those who surround us. Whilst this is applicable to all of us as we tread the path, this matter is especially emphasised when Leo is placed on the Ascendant of the natal chart.

In his classic work, *Beyond the Intellect*, Douglas Baker emphasises the importance of the archetype of Meaning and the instrumental role which this plays in our psychological and spiritual growth. Meaning itself is an archetype contributing energies

Mythological frieze sarcophagus showing the Labours of Hercules.
Ca. 240-250 AD. Rome, Palazzo Altemps (inv. 8642).

constantly into the conscious part of our psyche through our every word, each thought that we elaborate, and every action that we perform. When we are able to grasp the meaning of something, we perceive its underlying reality. The archetypal factor of meaning is especially important to those of us who meditate as we seek to gain understanding of ourselves, our motives and our behaviours. This enables us to discriminate between the real and the unreal whereby we may lead spiritually effective lives. Douglas Baker states here:

'One cannot be expected to perceive immediately truth, beauty and goodness in everything around one, but the intermediary of that holy three is meaning and that we should always search for. Out of that search there never fails to come, if it is persistent and habitual, access through direct perception to the divine.' [1]

In esoteric astrology meaning is ruled by Aries, Mercury and the 1st house of the chart. It is through the Rising Sign or Ascendant that the Soul imprints the personality at birth with a blueprint for its expression. The Rising Sign in the natal chart indicates our deepest potential and the prime source of our creative energy and wisdom. This emphasises the importance of the archetypal quality of meaning which is accentuated for those who have Aries located on the Ascendant in the natal chart. It is no coincidence that Mercury, the psychopomp, the aspect of the Higher Self which seeks to unite the personality to its intent, is related to this astrological archetype which exhorts us to learn to read the messages conveyed from within by the Soul as a means of leading us onwards on our spiritual journey. These can take the form of symbols in dreams and meditations, synchronicities in our daily lives and in events in life where the Soul is trying to communicate with us as a means of pointing us towards suitable avenues of spiritual expression.

The acquisition of meaning is an existential matter. When we study a poem, listen to music or observe a genuine work of art, it may inspire us and take us to an elevated level of consciousness, perhaps in accord with the level from which the creator of the work received their inspiration. However, it is the meaning that we obtain here which conveys the underlying reality to us. This is not confined merely to the meaning which the poet, composer or artist intended to express but rather what their work means to those who perceive it. It is important to remember that the very nature of the word 'meaning' implies an original intent. If we were to trace this to its source we would return to the divine word, the AUM which gave rise to our manifest universe as the transcendent being sounded forth the note of creation.

Mythology represents the great method which humanity has fashioned as a means of both discovering the nature of the archetypes and in utilising their evolutionary energies. The ancients portrayed the archetypal energies which impacted upon their lives by means of their pantheon of gods who were actively engaged in human events.

The Greeks used the exalted heights of Mount Olympus to symbolise the transcendental location of the archetypes which hover over humanity and which condition and influence our lives. Astrology has related the Greek and Roman gods to the planets within our solar system as a means of illustrating the effects of archetypal energies upon the human psyche and planetary life in general. As we have seen, the astrological chart represents a 'map of the psyche' which reveals both the nature and the effects of archetypal energies operative within our lives and the means by which we may utilise these for the purpose of attaining Psychosynthesis.

In Ancient Greece creative individuals were said to be inspired by the Muses. The Muses were the retinue of Apollo, the Sun God, who is symbolic of the solar or spiritual principle within. To be inspired by the muses means to be stirred from the levels of the Soul which, as we have seen, is the realm from which the archetypes are first expressed. Any true or genuine work of art arises through the artist gaining access to the creative energies of the superconscious whereby they are inspired from the archetypal realms of the Soul as they directly perceive what Plato described as truth, beauty and goodness. Creative individuals such as artists, poets and seers are inspired from these archetypal levels of the psyche.

When we tread the path we respond to the call within and awaken to our ultimate destiny. As stated previously, Joseph Campbell described this as 'the call to adventure'. Of particular importance to us here therefore, is the archetype of the Hero which is symbolised by the various hero myths of our world. There are numerous examples of this in mythology such as the aforementioned Labours of Hercules, the quest of Jason for the Golden Fleece, the knights questing for the Grail, the Voyages of Odysseus and the Adventures of Theseus, to name but a few.

The heroic qualities of those precious individuals who have successfully undertaken the evolutionary journey to the source of their being, as symbolised by the heroes of myth, have been absorbed into the unconscious whereby the morphic fields created by their endeavours feed those who tread the path today as they are required both to access and express the hero archetype. In the astrological natal chart this is indicated by the placement of Scorpio, its planetary ruler Mars and the 8th house which indicate the various tests and trials which will confront us whilst also advising us of the ways in which we may access and express heroic qualities for the purpose of overcoming these as a means of promoting spiritual growth.

Joseph Campbell defines the hero in the following way:

'The hero is one who, while still alive, knows and represents the claims of the superconsciousness which throughout creation is more or less unconscious. The adventure of the hero represents the moment in his life when he achieved illumination—the nuclear moment when, while still alive, he found and opened the road to the light beyond the dark walls of our living death.'[2]

Importantly, Jung described how the archetypes are represented in the human psyche as symbols, thereby offering us a means of obtaining guidance and direction from within. By studying and interpreting the symbols of myth we can gain insight into the archetypal forces which underlie human experience and that drive humanity forward towards the realisation of its spiritual purpose. Both Jung and Campbell were acutely aware of the important part which myth played in directing our consciousness towards wholeness. Campbell observed:

> '*It has always been the prime function of mythology and rite to supply the symbols that carry the human spirit forward, in counteraction to those other constant human fantasies that tend to tie it back.*'[3]

When treading the path we must be aware that we each possess our own psyche with its existential set of dynamics derived from archetypal forces. When we consider the symbols of myth we should ask ourselves what the various images mean in our own lives so that we may connect them to our own experiences rather than these being merely abstractions. We begin to discover myths which are very personal to us as we recognise their archetypal themes being expressed in our own life. Campbell believed that we should ascertain our own 'personal myth' which can serve towards both inspiring us whilst also enabling us to identify with, and express, the archetypal energies which it portrays.

CHAPTER 15

SYMBOLS AS REPRESENTATIONS
OF ARCHETYPES

WHEN WE TREAD THE PATH WE SEEK TO ALIGN our intent to that of the Soul. In seeking to become an effective instrument of spiritual expression we require guidance and direction from the Higher Self. But how do we obtain this? By what means does the immortal part of our being convey its intent to us? At what level of our being does such an interchange take place? And in what language does it occur?

Jung stated that archetypes are represented within the human psyche as symbols. Archetypes surface in our consciousness in symbolic form through our dreams and also through our meditations. Symbolic language enables the Soul to offer meaning and direction to us so that we may implement its objectives. Jung was aware that many dreams present the individual with images and associations that are analogous to primitive ideas, myths and rites which themselves are based upon humanity's attempts to both to understand and utilise the energies of the archetypes. He describes dreams as '*The soil from which most symbols organically grow.*'[1]

Originally the word symbol was used to refer to the two halves of an object, such as a stick or coin which had been broken in half by two individuals and the separate pieces then retained by each of them as evidence of the contract which they had entered into. A symbol was thus the missing part of an object which if placed together with its partner then had its original wholeness restored.[2]

Symbolic language is used by the Higher Self to develop our own wholeness of being as it enables us to function beyond the level of the intellect amidst the echelons of abstract thought. It leads us to the missing, but ever present, part of our being—the Higher Self. By developing our subjective resources and by nurturing the symbolic life we may receive direction and guidance from the Soul and become eligible to share in its energies and powers. By this process we accelerate the construction of the antakarana whose constituents are derived from the energies of the plane of Higher Manas. It is by virtue of the antakarana that the Soul and the personality can engage in symbolic dialogue so that the Higher Self may offer the personality guidance and direction towards implementing its intent.

As stated previously, the practice of abstract thought represents the current frontier in human consciousness. This level of awareness transcends that of the human intellect. As members of humanity we function competently in our application of intellect in our daily lives. Indeed in the Western world the intellect, whilst serving a most useful purpose which is particularly evident in the areas of science and technology, has sadly been over-developed at the expense of our higher faculties of abstract thought and intuition. By engaging in the practice of abstract thought we are able to liberate our minds from kama-manas. This is a very important factor in treading the path whereby we can free ourselves from the dominion of the astral body thereby assisting us towards transmuting the energies of the solar plexus chakra into those of the heart chakra and the energies of the sacral chakra into those of the throat.

The objective of Jung's individuation process is to unify the conscious and unconscious contents of the psyche and in doing so, to

Aegeus and Themis, Altes Museum

give birth to what he described as the 'transcendent function of the psyche'. This enables the Self to fully realise its potential. Symbolism plays a most important part in this process. Heinrich Zimmer had a long-standing relationship with Jung whilst also serving as both a friend and mentor to Joseph Campbell. On the subject of symbolism Zimmer states:

> '... for the ultimate and real task of philosophy, according to Indian thought, and to such classical Occidental philosophers as Plato, transcends the power and task of reason. Access to truth demands a passage beyond the compass of ordered thought. And by the same token: the teaching of transcendent truth cannot be by logic, but only by pregnant paradox and by symbol and image. Where a carefully reasoned thinker, progressing step by step, would be forced to halt (out of breath, as it were, at the confines of the stratosphere, panting for lack of oxygen, swooning with pulmonary and cardiac distress) the mind can still go on. The mind can soar and enter the supernal sphere on the wings of symbols, which represent the truth beyond the pairs of opposites, eluding by those

*wings the bird-net of the basic principle of earthbound human logic,
the pedestrian principle of the incompatibility of opposites. For
what 'transcendent' means is the transcending (among other things)
of the bounding and basic logical laws of the human mind.'*[3]

It was illustrated in Chapter 11, when we considered the factor of
maya as the 'veil of the goddess', that all that is manifest within nature
contains an opposite, and that the spiritual aspirant seeks to attain a
state of unity which both underlies and transcends the duality of
manifestation. Jung writes:

> *'The general function of dreams is to try to restore our
> psychological balance by producing dream material that re-
> establishes, in a subtle way, the total psychic equilibrium. This is
> what I call the complementary (or compensatory) role of dreams
> in our psychic make-up.'*[4]

Jung emphasised that the symbols offered to us through our dreams
are natural attempts to reconcile and unite opposites within our psyche.
The basis of his psychotherapy was to establish the relationship of the
ego with the Self. Ultimately, this leads one to a level of being which
transcends the dualistic nature of the manifest world. Towards these
ends the Soul utilises symbolism as a means of conveying its intent to
the personality so that we may lead our lives accordingly.

Jung stated that those who hold unrealistic ideas or possess elevated
opinions of themselves, or who devise grandiose plans which are
disproportionate to their actual capacities, are likely to dream of flying
or falling. He also emphasised that recurring dreams normally serve a
similar function for the individual concerned. Jung states here that:

> *'The dream compensates for the deficiencies of their personalities, and
> at the same time it warns them of the dangers in their present course.'*[5]

Dreams are common to the entire human race and provide the perfect
opportunity for the Higher Self to communicate with us when the
vehicles of the personality are stilled. As well as offering us guidance

and direction the Soul may also employ symbolic imagery as a means of providing us with creative inspiration. History is littered with examples of this. The German organic chemist August Kekule derived his understanding of the molecular structure of benzene as a closed carbon ring when the esoteric symbol of the Ouroboros[6] appeared to him in a dream. Niels Bohr dreamt of a day at a race course then realized that the marked lanes on the track symbolised the fixed and specific orbits that electrons are required to follow as they circulate around atomic nuclei and Elias Howe, who invented the sewing machine, dreamt of cannibals who had tossed him into a pot for the purpose of cooking him alive. When he tried to escape he was forced back into the cauldron by the sharp points of their spears which contained holes within them. Upon waking, he realized the answer to the problem of design which he had been seeking in that he should move the thread transport hole down to the point of the needle.

In Greek mythology Asclepius was the god of healing. There was a famous temple built in his honour at Epidaurus. The method of healing practised at this shrine was based upon dreams. The sick that arrived at the temple were clothed in pristine white garments. Ritual purification and offerings occurred prior to the supplicants sleeping in the most sacred area of temple on couches situated under a statue of the god. It was believed that Asclepius would manifest and prescribe a cure to the sufferer whilst they slept. The percentage of recoveries from illness amongst the sick who attended the temple was said to be unusually high for that period in time.

If we are able to understand the language of the unconscious whose characters are the symbols communicated to us primarily through our dreams, and also through our meditations, we are then able to obtain direction and guidance from the Higher Self and thereby lead a spiritually effective life. We should therefore remain both open and receptive to the symbolic imagery which the Higher Self is seeking to communicate to us.

Whenever we think, we do so in symbolic terms; streams of images appear within our mind. These determine the flow of our thoughts. Symbolic language therefore represents a natural way in which the Soul can communicate with us.

All images which the Higher Self feeds us are derived from our own personal experience. This constitutes what psychology refers to as our 'ex-externa'. The ancients were aware of this factor and held the belief that 'memory is the mother of the muses'. In Chapter 11 we considered the factor of maya and how the myriad forms contained within our world, and our experiences in life, are of a transient nature and that they obscure the underlying One Divine Life. It is a most fascinating esoteric fact however that the forms which we have perceived, and the experiences which we have undergone, can be utilised by the Soul in innumerable combinations in the form of symbolic imagery. This occurs by virtue of the Soul projecting images from the collective unconscious onto a region of the mental body which is organized around a centre that coincides with the pineal gland. It is here that the mental body functions as a receptor for images located in the collective unconscious, the personal unconscious and within our aura. The images are projected through passages at the astral level where they may be clothed with emotional affect before finding the closest corresponding images to those which are stored in the memory banks of the brain at etheric, rather than physical, levels.

On this basis, we are thereby provided with our own existential language of the unconscious which can offer us guidance and direction in our lives whereby we may fulfil the intent of the transcendent aspect of our being—the Higher Self amidst the maya of the lower worlds.

Jung emphasised the symbol-making propensity of the human psyche and that consciousness served the purpose of not merely recognizing and assimilating the contents of the external world by means of the five senses, but also in utilising these as symbols for the purpose of translating into visible reality the contents of the world within. Importantly, Jung stated that symbols are spontaneous and autonomous productions of the psyche and that we do not create our symbols, but that rather we discover them. Symbols emanate from the realms of consciousness where the Soul resides (Atma, Buddhi and Manas) as it strives to make us aware of archetypal factors at play in our lives which can assist us towards expressing its intent. On the nature of symbols Jung writes:

'*... any word or image is symbolic, or becomes a symbol, when it implies something more than its obvious and immediate meaning... it has a wider unconscious aspect that is never precisely defined or fully explained ... As the mind explores the symbol, it is led to ideas that lie beyond the grasp of reason.*'[7]

A sign represents something which is known. However, a symbol is an image or representation indicating something which is unknown or mysterious. Unlike a sign which conveys abstract, objective meaning, a symbol imparts living, dynamic, subjective meaning. This meaning constantly changes.

Symbols both release and transform psychic energy. They have the capacity to raise us from the level of our instincts and our psychological drives which bind us to the maya-driven merry-go-round of material existence, to a position of spiritual expression. When we seek to develop and express our spirituality we should therefore remain both open and receptive to the symbolic imagery which the Higher Self is seeking to communicate to us.

A symbol is dynamic. The moment that we focus upon it, it begins to change. A symbol adapts itself to us and to the meaning that it is trying to convey. It is existential. A symbol is dynamic both in terms of what is known of it and what remains to be known of it. We cannot know everything there is to know about any particular symbol. Jung stated that a symbol cannot be drained of its meaning. Anyone who has embarked upon a serious study of either their own dream symbolism, or that of others, is aware of that there is a marked contextual element here. Jung writes:

'*No dream symbol can be separated from the individual who dreams it, and there is no definite or straightforward interpretation of any dream.*'[8]

Dream interpretation varies, depending upon the level of our being which the corresponding archetype is seeking to inform us about. When interpreting symbols we must be aware of their different layers of meaning and of how the same symbol can offer different or existential meaning to the one who perceives it. This meaning too can change depending upon the context in which the symbol is placed. Mercury is the psychopomp, but he is also the ruler of quicksilver, and as quickly as we pursue the meaning of symbols so they can just as easily slip out of our grasp.

Each of us must search within our own unconscious for our own existential symbols. There will be instances in our subjective lives where we are offered symbols that are personal to us, perhaps the emergence of a figure from our childhood, or an incident related to an earlier event in our lives. The challenge is for us to recognise and interpret the language of the Soul as a means of ascertaining its purpose and intent. It is here that we require our spiritual faculties of intuition and abstract thought.

Nevertheless, there are many symbols that possess a general meaning. Jung described these as 'motifs' although he did stress that these, like other symbols, must be considered within the context of the dream itself, rather than as being self-explanatory.

The symbol of the cave is usually held to represent something of a subjective nature which may be located at deep and/or hidden levels of our psyche. The content of a cave is obscured from public view hence this symbol may also suggest a need for us to engage in a process of withdrawal from our engagement with the transitory affairs of the mundane world in favour of our spiritual development. This symbol may also allude to the 'cave of the heart' and its dark chamber where the light of spirit emerges. This is the realm of our being which we enter in meditation.

A contemporary dream symbol is that of the motor car which represents the personality as the vehicle of the Soul. The condition of the car which we happen to be driving, our ability towards controlling the car in pursuing the appropriate direction, our adherence to the Highway Code, are all factors which we must take into account in terms of our relationship to the Soul and our ability to carry out its intent. Another frequently occurring dream symbol depicting the personality is that of the house: the condition of the house, our location within a particular room of a house and its general condition can be most revealing. Similarly, the contents, size and relationship of the rooms within the house to each other may be held to symbolize various components of functions of the psyche and their interaction. If we are located within the basement it is suggestive of the hidden realms of our psyche. A process of exploration and cleansing within the lower realms of our psyche may be implied here including the lower unconscious and the repressed complexes and aspects of the Dweller on the Threshold which are located at astro-mental levels. However, in the process of removing the unwanted contents found here we may also discover items which are of great value to us which relate to the superconscious—the realms of Atma, Buddhi and Manas. If we are in the kitchen preparing food then it may indicate that we possess the capacity to offer nourishment to others in the form of spiritual teachings.

We shall now consider appropriate steps which we can take when seeking counsel with the Higher Self by virtue of dream symbolism.

Firstly, we should equip ourselves with a sufficient vocabulary of symbols to enable the Higher Self to communicate with us. Douglas Baker frequently stated that the human mind is like a typewriter keyboard and it must be well stocked to allow meaningful dialogue to occur. The study of mythology, literature, poetry and travel are effective ways of assisting this process. The importance of the study of mythology cannot be over-emphasised by virtue of the fact that myths are representations of archetypes and, as Jung illustrated, it is common for us to perceive underlying mythic themes when we observe our dreams over a period of time.

Secondly, we should cultivate the ability to sleep lightly. By achieving this we create a longer period of time in which the psychopomp can communicate with us (early nights and the use of an alarm clock to break up our sleep patterns can assist here). The lighter we can sleep, the more likely we are to register that which emanates from within. The state between sleep and waking called hypnopompia is the most effective time for conscious contact with the Higher Self. The other important time is when dropping off to sleep which is referred to as hypnogogia. We should seek to extend these two periods by sleeping lightly. In relation to the state of hypnopompia Douglas Baker believed that:

'This is a most receptive period. The waking dream especially is of importance and, in the absence of meditation, is about the only opportunity available to the Higher Self to impress its vehicles with any sort of communication.'[9]

Thirdly, it is important to bear in mind that the Higher Self is best able to impress symbolic meaning upon the individual who is able to exert control over their various thoughts and desires. C. W. Leadbeater in his work entitled *Dreams: What They Are and How They are Caused* illustrated that, as well as the Soul, there are other factors operative in the production of dreams. He described how the fluctuating energies and currents of the astral world impact upon the astral counterpart of the physical brain which then modifies these energies according to its content. This can exert powerful effects upon the dream life whilst bearing no relationship to the intent which the Soul is seeking to convey to us.

Meditation serves towards stilling the personality vehicles and, in particular, calming and disciplining the astral body. The regular practice of meditation enhances the capacity of the Soul towards offering us symbolic meaning by virtue of our dreams whilst simultaneously strengthening and widening the antakarana.

Leadbeater also illustrated that in the sleep state, the physical brain possesses a tendency to express stimuli in the surrounding outer world in pictorial form, whilst the workings of the etheric counterpart of the brain, containing its memory banks, must also be considered here. Just as a region of the mental body corresponding to the pineal gland acts as a receptor for images found within the unconscious, there is located here a selector mechanism. When we enter the sleep state the flow of random images which often stream through consciousness arise from the brain losing its selector capacity whereby the most recent images stored in its etheric memory banks tend to produce what in the Orient are referred to as 'vrittis'.

The quality of discrimination is therefore most important as we must discern between those dreams which emanate from the Higher Self and those which do not. On this matter Douglas Baker writes in his classic work *The Psychology of Discipleship*:

'There is an attitude current in esoteric circles that all dreams are reflections of the truth. The disciple has to learn that in many instances they are not and that it takes years to learn to separate the real from the unreal in the dream experience. The matter is complicated by the fact that as the disciple integrates their personality, its various elements become more independent, more energised and more vociferous! Each little 'I' becomes more powerful that it adds its voice and opinions to the dream content, attracting to itself images and symbols vibrating to its own separate note.

'It is only when the disciple has first accomplished personality integration and added to it the elimination of ego that these satellite personalities[10] fall away from the dreamlife; the art of dreaming becomes one of the disciple's newly-won accomplishments as part of the art of equipping himself.'[11]

It is also important to be aware that when we tread the path we also confront the Dweller on the Threshold frequently in our dream life. The slow attrition of the Dweller, which occurs through the undertaking of spiritual disciplines, leads to increased clarity in terms of dream content as the purpose of the Soul is revealed to us in symbolic language.

The erosion of the Dweller is greatly assisted by the keeping of a spiritual diary wherein we should record our dreams, the results of our meditations and our general spiritual endeavours. This provides a focal point for the Higher Self and serves towards establishing a dialogue between Soul and personality. The Spiritual Diary may be viewed as our altar which we approach with reverence as we seek to commune with the immortal aspect of our being. A well maintained spiritual diary allows us to observe any specific themes which occur in our dream life.

Douglas Baker writes:

'With the assistance of a spiritual diary, it should be possible for the neophyte to accumulate through the passage of say, five or ten, or even fifteen years, a comprehensive list of many hundreds of symbols with their related meanings.'[12]

Jung also demonstrated that symbols are not exclusive to one's dream life. He outlined how symbols may appear in all manner of psychic manifestations. There are symbolic thoughts and feelings and symbolic acts and situations.

Symbols also manifest in our lives by a process which Jung called synchronicity. This term refers to a 'meaningful coincidence' of objective and subjective events which themselves are not causally related. Synchronicity suggests the presence of an underlying archetype seeking expression through the individual concerned. When we consider the principle of hylozoism, that 'all things live within the body of a greater being' and that 'all life is interconnected' then it is logical to assume an interrelationship between the human psyche and the external world.

Throughout the ages members of humanity have sought and discovered various methods towards effecting spiritual transformation. If the methods contained within the practices related to these were successful, then they opened the floodgates to higher levels of consciousness. Such techniques were required to affect not only a synthesis between personality and Soul but to also be applicable to the contemporary challenges related to the treading of the spiritual path and to the human condition in its present state. In Chapter 10, I illustrated how these are described as Keys to the Mysteries.

Douglas Baker was instrumental in developing esoteric or soul-centred Astrology as a Key to the Mysteries for the 21st century and beyond, following on from the pioneering work of Carl Jung and his concept of archetypes and their representation within the human psyche as symbols. Esoteric astrology enables the Soul or Higher Self to offer guidance and direction to the personality as a means of it ascertaining and implementing its purpose through the use of symbolic language.

Esoteric astrology employs a language of the unconscious relating the archetypal energy contained in astrological symbols to images received in dreams and meditation. The horoscope indicates our existential nature and the purpose of the Soul. It can also relate us to the meaning of our existential symbols. This enables a symbolic dialogue to occur between the Higher Self and the personality. This serves towards constructing the antakarana whilst allowing the Soul to guide the personality towards suitable areas of expression. In this respect Douglas Baker observes:

'*Only through esoteric astrology, derived from initiate teachings of the most ancient origin, can the links between original meaning and the present-day function of symbols be comprehended. In other, equally ancient keys, like Alchemy, correlations between symbol and meaning have become obscure.*'[13]

It is on this basis that Dr Baker compiled his magnum opus, the three volume *Douglas Baker's Dictionary of Astrology for the Twenty First Century* whereby he provides us with a comprehensive 'language of the unconscious.' In Volume One he provides an immediate and complete reference to the vast majority of words in the English language as they convert to their astrological equivalent. In Volumes Two and Three the reverse format is given with astrological aspects translated into English words and phrases. We shall now consider a basic example of how this form of astrology works:

In astrology, bridges, including the antakarana, are related to the sign of Libra and astrologically Libra rules relationships and partnerships. Where Libra and Uranus are placed in a horoscope, together with the influences upon the 7th house, this will describe what kind of partnerships will develop in our lives. The ultimate partnership is that with our Higher Self. When Libra is placed on the Ascendant in the natal chart additional emphasis is placed upon the construction of the antakarana as a means of relating to the Soul although this process is fundamental towards treading the path. The building of the antakarana is greatly assisted by the keeping of a spiritual diary which also comes under the domain of the Libran astrological archetype.

An example of a relevant dream here would be of a bridge that was blocked by the branches of a Willow tree making it very difficult to cross. Willow is the Bach Flower Remedy for those suffering with resentment. The bridge/antakarana cannot be crossed by someone full of resentment. In this dream the Higher Self is not only highlighting a factor in one's life which is constricting one's spiritual growth, but is also offering a solution.

This represents only a most rudimentary illustration of a means of bridging the current frontier of human consciousness through the practice of abstract thought. I would recommend Carl Jung's book *Man and his Symbols*, Douglas Baker's aforementioned three volume *Douglas Baker's Dictionary of Astrology for the Twenty First Century*, and his work *Beyond the Intellect* for the purpose of one deriving insight into this most important key towards enabling a symbolic dialogue to occur between Soul and personality.

CHAPTER 16

THE PSYCHOPOMP

WHEN WE TREAD THE SPIRITUAL PATH THE SOUL employs various ways in offering us spiritual meaning as we endeavour to ascend the symbolic cliff-face of the mountain of initiation. The aspect of the Soul that assists us in our endeavours here is referred to as the Psychopomp . The psychopomp seeks to unite the personality with the intent of the Higher Self. Just as Sherpa Tenzing served as Sir Edmund Hilary's guide in his ground-breaking ascent of Mount Everest, so the psychopomp assists us with its knowledge and experience of the inner terrain which we must traverse as we proceed on our evolutionary journey. We all require assistance in the form of meaning and direction as we tread the symbolic mountain path. It is here that we encounter the many challenges which relate to the transformation of the base metal of the transient, corruptible human personality, together with its associated impurities, into the shining, radiant, eternal, incorruptible gold of the Soul.

The word psychopomp is derived from the Greek language, literally meaning 'guide of souls'. In Greek mythology the psychopomp is symbolised by Hermes, the messenger of the gods, whose Roman equivalent is Mercury. It is important to bear in mind that the various gods of myth are in essence personifications of the energies and qualities of the unconscious that Jung referred to as archetypes. As we have seen these are instrumental to the processes of evolution.

As well as conducting Souls into the afterlife, the Greek god Hermes conveys information from the gods situated on Mount Olympus (a symbol of the transcendent realm and the location of the archetypes) to the world of mortals. Hermes wears a winged helmet and sandals which represents the capacity to engage in flights of consciousness. He carries the caduceus which serves as a magic wand enabling him to serve as an intermediary between the mortal and the divine realms. In respect of its symbolism Douglas Baker writes:

'Hermes carries the caduceus which combines the chthonic principle of the serpent and the aerial principle of the bird. Birds are the symbol for spiritual potential and the caduceus is the symbol for spiritual potential within. The winged helmet and sandals together with the caduceus therefore symbolise the capacity of the psychopomp to function as a mediator between the conscious and the unconscious realms of the human psyche.'[1]

The psychopomp relates the unconscious realms of the human psyche to those of a conscious nature. Its subjective nature may be expressed through art, music, poetry and other creative pursuits. Our experiences here may serve to elevate our consciousness and provide us with inspiration and meaning. In its role as a divine messenger the psychopomp functions primarily through the medium of symbol. As we have seen, symbolic language is instrumental in the process of spiritual transformation and enables the Soul to offer meaning and direction to the personality so that it may implement its purpose. This work has demonstrated that symbolic language occurs mainly through dreams, meditation and by virtue of synchronicities in accord with the role of Hermes who is the god of revelation and the bringer of dreams.

Mercury and Argus by Diego Velazquez

The individual human psyche possesses its own unique qualities and we each experience the psychopomp in our own existential way. Initially, the inner guide tends to manifest in dream scenarios as a member of the opposite sex. Jung referred to this as the anima for males and the animus for females. Hermes also leads living Souls to the underworld, or inner worlds, including Orpheus in his search for Eurydice. This symbolises the spiritual seeker's efforts towards uniting with the anima.

The sea is held to be the great symbol of the collective unconscious. It is common for us to experience dreams where an alluring and enticing female figure appears to us if we are male, or an attractive, handsome, courageous man if we are female. These are a representation of the psychopomp which, through the mechanism of symbol, is beckoning us into an exploration of the inner worlds and all that this entails. The anima of a man may serve as an inspirational muse, whilst the animus of a woman may function as a heroic figure leading one upwards to the spiritual realms.

Depending on the development and the awareness of the individual, the anima can also be the femme fatale or seductress who lures one away from the essence of one's being towards the transient matters of the outer world. These are concealed under the guise of love and bliss but only serve towards engaging one further in the realms of maya. This dangerous aspect of the anima is represented in myth by the Greek Sirens and the German Lorelei. The animus too possesses negative characteristics. The Greek myth relating to the Abduction of Persephone may be held to symbolise here certain animus qualities which lure the woman away from human relationships, and particularly those with the opposite sex. It is also a most common occurrence whereby we project the numinous qualities of the anima or animus onto prospective partners whose human frailties cannot possibly satisfy our expectations here.

After the anima, or animus phase of the psychopomp's expression, its role is thereafter assumed by a spiritual mentor or guru in the outer world. The psychopomp can adopt the form of such a spiritual teacher as a means of conveying its intent to us through our dreams; the phase of the teacher or guru is eventually replaced by us finding our own existential inner guide. This expression of the Higher Self is not related to the spirit guides whom mediums seek contact with.

As I stated in the first chapter, Carl Jung was fascinated by the subject of alchemy. He was well aware of the instrumental role which the psychopomp plays here and the various symbolic guises which it adopts in its role as an agent of spiritual transformation. He writes:

'From the earliest times, Hermes was the mystagogue and psychopomp of the alchemists, their friend and counsellor, who leads them to the goal of their work. He is like a teacher mediating between the stone and the disciple.[2] To others the friend appears in the shape of Christ or Khidr[3] or a visible or invisible guru, or some other personal guide or leader figure.'[4]

It is important to note that in Greek myth, despite his capacity to mediate between the mortal and immortal realms, Hermes is also a trickster. This advises us to take care when receiving and analysing the contents of the unconscious which are revealed to us through our dreams and our meditations. It is important that we develop the quality of discrimination here in discerning between that which emanates from the Soul and that which is simply the product of our imaginings and the effects of the astral plane.

CHAPTER 17

THE ANTAKARANA

A S I HAVE SHOWN, SPIRITUAL DEVELOPMENT consists of us constructing the antakarana or rainbow bridge which links Soul and personality. Through our various endeavours to express the qualities of the Soul, as a means of unfolding its symbolic petals, we begin to build this bridge to the higher worlds. When the antakarana strengthens and widens, through our spiritual practice and efforts, we are also able to radiate spiritual energies outwards to the rest of humanity whereby we act as channels stimulating the spiritual growth of others.

When we tread the spiritual path we are seeking to reach the Fifth Kingdom of Souls. This consists of perfected beings or masters who have successfully trodden this path having undergone and successfully overcome every challenge that life in human form has to offer as a means of unfolding the flower of the Soul. In our efforts to reach the Fifth Kingdom we are assisted by our study of the occult classics and by rendering acts of service to humanity. In seeking to construct the antakarana it is of particular assistance to undertake the regular practice of meditation where energy from the Higher Self is passed down to the personality via this bridgehead. Conversely, through the practice of meditation we widen and strengthen the antakarana so that we may more easily access the energies of the Fifth Kingdom. This provides us with the necessary vitality, momentum and strength towards serving humanity and, ultimately, to reach the Fifth Kingdom ourselves.

The two principal attributes of meditation are those of *energy* and *meaning*. These are of profound importance to one who is seeking to scale the symbolic cliff-face of the mountain of spiritual initiation. Douglas Baker states:

> '*It is through creative meditation, which draws on ever-changing images surfacing from the sea of the unconscious, that life can be truly understood. To examine it from without is but to examine its shadow.*'[1]

When we undertake the practice of meditation we seek to establish a perfect alignment of the physical, astral and mental bodies, and to develop contact with the Higher Self so that we may express the archetypal patterns found on the planes of consciousness where the Soul resides. In doing so we may then yoke ourselves to the consciousness of the greater being within which we reside—the Planetary Logos.

This is not the place to expound any particular method of meditation as there are numerous and voluminous works relating to this practice. However, if you are seeking guidance here then the consulting of the *Yoga Sutras of Patanjali*, or any of the many commentaries on this classic work are recommended. Douglas Baker's two books *Meditation: The Theory and Practice* and *Superconsciousness Through Meditation* offers the reader a simple and concise exposition relating to both the theory and practice of this 'language of the god's which serves to construct the antakarana.

The antakarana is constructed from the energies of the plane of Higher Manas. It is the bridge between the higher mind and its lower

Jacob's Ladder by William Blake

counterpart—the human intellect. Importantly, as we have seen, it is through the antakarana that a dialogue can be established between the Soul and the personality, allowing the Soul to offer guidance to the personality through the symbolism that occurs in dreams and meditation.

Meditation is also an existential matter in that there are as many ways to meditate as there are meditators! It is of fundamental importance here, however, to be aware that through the regular practice of meditation we are constructing the antakarana whilst also depositing energies into the cosmic bank of the Soul for future use both in this particular life, and in our subsequent incarnations. It is also essential here that we do not judge meditation by its apparent results: spiritual development occurs at great depth and is not necessarily seen on the surface. Rather, it is best to adopt the practice of meditation and persist with it in the knowledge that we are depositing energy at a spiritual level, and that we shall eventually reap the reward here.

The practice of abstract thought represents the current frontier of human consciousness. The savage Lemurian civilisation established the physical body and opened the sacral chakra of humanity upon this planet. The succeeding Atlantean civilisation served to fashion the astral body whilst opening the solar plexus chakra of humanity. Our current Aryan Root Race exists for the purpose of developing the mental body and, in doing so, opening the throat chakra of humanity. At present, the mental body of humanity is only half-formed. It functions most competently in terms of the four lowest seven mental sub-planes which relate to the expression of intellect. Jung was aware of the limitations of the human intellect as simply an aspect and a function of the psyche which extends inestimably beyond the boundaries of ordinary waking consciousness.

The widening and strengthening of the antakarana serves to increasingly channel the energies of the Higher Self into the aura of the personality suffusing it with spiritual qualities. This includes those which have been hard won in previous lives where they have passed from the personality up the antakarana to be stored in the permanent atoms of the Soul where they serve towards unfolding its symbolic lotus petals.

In the early part of the Soul's evolutionary sojourn through the human kingdom the antakarana is a tenuous thread linking the Higher Self and its personality. As the Soul progresses from the Mutable to the Fixed Cross, and especially upon negotiating the Cardinal Cross, the antakarana strengthens and widens to the extent that we may access vast reservoirs of spiritual energy. This is a prelude to the culmination of the Soul's endeavours when the antakarana ceases to exist as the personality becomes completely Soul-infused.

The antakarana has been symbolically represented in various forms of myth. In the Biblical Book of Genesis it is symbolised by Jacob's Ladder which he envisioned during his flight from his brother Esau. Jacob dreamt of a ladder on the Earth reaching upwards to heaven and upon which angels were ascending and descending; as we tread the path we construct our very own Jacob's Ladder whilst also contributing to the building of the planetary antakarana.

In Norse Myth the antakarana is depicted as Bifrost, the rainbow bridge connecting Asgard, the realm of the gods, to Midgard the realm inhabited by humanity. The word Bifrost, which is of Icelandic origin, means 'shimmering path'. This is an apt description for the structure which links humanity to the causal realms of existence and which provides us with the capacity to access and express the energies and qualities of these particular levels of consciousness.

In Greek mythology the antakarana is symbolised by Ariadne's Thread. This enables the hero Theseus to escape from the labyrinth after slaying the Minotaur, which is half-man and half-beast. In this myth the hero Theseus symbolises the individual on the path. The maze represents the labyrinthine realms of the human psyche and also the lower worlds of maya within which our divine essence, the monad, is challenged towards realising its latent potential. Ariadne represents the psychopomp in the form of the anima. Her thread is wound up in a ball, a spherical shape symbolising the wholeness of being which the questing hero seeks. The Minotaur who guards the centre of the maze represents our lower nature (including the Dweller on the Threshold) and instincts, which we must overcome if we are to achieve spiritual transformation. The centre of the maze, which the Minotaur obscures, symbolises the centre of our being: the Higher Self.[2]

CHAPTER 18

THE GRAIL LEGEND AND THE SPIRITUAL PATH

A S I HAVE SHOWN THROUGHOUT THIS WORK, THE various myths of our world symbolise archetypal processes. We have already seen that archetypes, as divine ideas, govern and conduct the process of evolution.

In our study of the dynamics of myth we should be aware that the drama contained therein is a constant factor amidst the endeavours of humanity towards realising its spiritual potential. When we study myth we are both exploring, and gaining an understanding of the dynamics of the human psyche. As we have seen, the metaphors contained within the hero myths of our world provide us with deep insight into the trials and tribulations of the spiritual path and of the archetypal forces at play when we embark upon the inner journey. We shall now consider the Grail Legend as a means of illustration here.

The concept of the Holy Grail arose out of Celtic myth and was later infused by the teachings of mystical Christianity. The Grail is a vessel described as possessing magical properties. It offers healing, bliss and spiritual transformation to those who display the necessary qualities required to attain it. The Grail is situated in an otherworldly, or inner, realm of being. It may only be attained by the questing knight who possesses the necessary purity whilst displaying courage, heroism, honour and virtue as he overcomes the various challenges which confront him in pursuit of the sacred vessel. Immediately, one can perceive similarities between the Grail and the Soul, as the instrument of the monad, this being the integrating factor within the human psyche which Jung referred to as the Self. The Grail is a receptacle capable of receiving the divine energies of the monad which, at the third initiation, are increasingly poured into the vessel of the Soul.

La Queste del Saint Graal (The Quest for the Holy Grail) formed part of *The Vulgate Cycle*, a series of five prose volumes which describe the life of King Arthur and the quest for the Grail in magnificent detail. Whilst there are few conclusive answers as to its authorship, its major parts were compiled in the early 13th century. It was this work which created Galahad, the virgin knight who was destined to achieve the Grail. *The Vulgate Cycle* also served as a major source for Sir Thomas Mallory's classic work *Le Morte D'Arthur* which was written in the latter half of the 15th century.

In the Grail legend a stone with a sword embedded in it appears in the river near Camelot. The sword contains an inscription stating that only the greatest knight can draw the sword from the stone. King Arthur's established knights then attempt to extract the sword from the stone but none of them are able to achieve this. Sir Galahad, who had been knighted the day before, then proceeds to remove the sword from the stone. He is then able to occupy the Siege Perilous, this being the seat at the Round Table, reserved by Merlin the magician (a representation of the psychopomp), for the knight destined to achieve the Grail. It is fatal for any other knight to occupy this seat.

Galahad symbolises spiritual purity, heroism, honour and virtue of the highest degree. These are essential qualities if the neophyte is to ascend to the spiritual heights. It is only when we possess such qualities, allied to a fully integrated personality, that the Soul may then extract the sword of personality from the stone of material entrenchment and all that binds us to the Wheel of Rebirth, including our attachments and our various desires.

Galahad's ability to fill the Siege Perilous, thereby completing the Fellowship of Knights seated at the Round Table, demonstrates his capacity both to embrace and to utilise the forces of the unconscious. The circular form of the Round Table may be viewed as a mandala and therefore as a representation of the psychological wholeness which the individual engaged upon the spiritual quest is seeking. Jung considered the Self, as the integrating factor within the human psyche, to be expressed in mandala images. The Sanskrit word mandala means 'circle', a symbol of wholeness, unity and infinity.

When the Grail knights are assembled at the Round Table they obtain a partial vision of the Grail and they are each permitted to partake of its food. Each knight then vows to go in quest of the Grail so that they may understand its mystery. They each leave behind their noble and honourable lives at Camelot and enter the Forest Adventurous at their own chosen point, where the forest was darkest and where there was no pathway.

The partial vision of the Grail and the food supplied by it represents the stage of human evolution where the personality has become sufficiently aligned to the Soul to enable an impression to be made of the glory and ineffable bliss of the Higher Self. This is the first initiation as described by the wisdom teachings. This occurs after we experience divine unrest whereby the transient affairs of the outer world begin to lose their lustre and attraction as the pull of the monad exerts its effect.

We are transformed by this subjective experience in that our perception of life and of the objective world no longer remains the same. The treading of the path increasingly becomes a 'magnificent obsession' whereby all other aspects of our life, our wealth and possessions, career, social status, and all of the other trappings of maya are rendered as meaningless. This is symbolised by the knight's departure from Camelot in pursuit of the Grail. Similarly, when we seek spiritual transformation we must be prepared to leave our previous life behind and to relinquish any attachments in our lives,

*The Arming and Departure of the Knights. Number 2 of the Holy Grail
tapestries woven by Morris & Co. 1891-94 for Stanmore Hall.*

whether physical, emotional or mental, together with any other factors
which effectively bind us to the Wheel of Rebirth.

Joseph Campbell illustrates how the heroes of myth respond to the
'call to adventure' and thereafter venture forth into distant and
dangerous lands that symbolise the realms of the unconscious, where
they encounter many tests and trials which determine their right to
proceed further upon their quest and ultimately to attain their goal. In
the Arthurian Legends it is the partial vision of the Grail obtained by
the knights which represents the call to adventure. The Forest
Adventurous symbolises the uncharted territory of the human psyche
where the neophyte must enter, explore and embrace the various
challenges therein as a means of effecting spiritual transformation.

Upon attainment of the Grail the Fisher King or Wounded King is
healed and his kingdom is redeemed. This was previously a blighted
landscape referred to as the 'wasteland' where water would not flow
and which was thus bereft of vegetation. The king had been wounded
in the thighs (a euphemism for the genitals) by what is referred to as
the 'Dolorous Stroke'. This prevented the king from participating in
sovereign union with the land thus giving rise to the benighted
landscape.

The wounding of the Grail king and the resulting loss of sovereignty symbolises the challenges and the constraints that physical incarnation places upon our spiritual nature. The monad is effectively wounded and handicapped in terms of its true and full expression whereby dominion over the land is sought. The symbolic redemption of the wasteland occurs when the monad is able to attain its objective of developing and expressing its hitherto latent spiritual qualities through the acquisition of spiritual staying power. This is of course achieved by one successfully treading the path whereby one becomes a perfected instrument of spiritual expression, which here is symbolised by the Grail knight Galahad whose worthiness is demonstrated in his various adventures in quest of the sacred vessel.

Joseph Campbell considered the wasteland of the Grail legends to symbolise what he described as an *'inauthentic life'*. He is referring here to the need for us to access and express the qualities of the Higher Self, rather than merely leading a life limited by socio-cultural constraints whereby we conform to such dictates at the expense of pursuing a course of action which is in accord with the intent of the Soul.

In esoteric astrology the sign of Sagittarius, its planetary ruler the Earth and the 9th house of the natal chart rule the spiritual quest together with the capacity to obtain extensions in consciousness. The symbolic arrows of aspiration associated with this sign enable its adherents to penetrate beyond their existing psycho-spiritual horizons. Sagittarius also rules the matter of orientation. When treading the path it is essential that we pursue the correct course of action. This is achieved by us following our own existential pathway in life. This is especially emphasised when Sagittarius is placed on the Ascendant in the natal chart although the correct expression of this astrological archetype is applicable to us all as we seek to orient ourselves to the intent of the Soul. There are many ways of attaining the symbolic summit of the mountain and we must decide upon the various teachings and practices which we shall adopt as a means of attaining our goal. It is important to bear in mind here that as members of humanity we are all unique individuals with our own existential development, history and purpose.

In the Grail myth, as Campbell demonstrates, this is symbolised by the manner in which each of the Grail knights enters the Forest Adventurous, as previously described. This symbolises the unique nature of the process of spiritual transformation for each and every one of us.

The Forest Adventurous in Grail Mythology, Symbol of Spiritual Transformation.
The Temptation of Sir Perceval by Arthur Hacker

CHAPTER 19

PRINCIPLES OF PSYCHOSYNTHESIS

W E MAY TAKE AN IMPORTANT STEP ON OUR spiritual journey by recognising that everything emanates from within. The innermost aspect of our being, the monad, is divine, and from this deific source there flows into our mind inspiration, aspiration, altruism, love, wisdom, compassion, self-sacrifice and all other factors which can ennoble both ourselves and humanity. Spirituality is related to the effort which we place into raising the consciousness of all of the kingdoms of life surrounding us. This should include us engaging in the nurturing of plants, displaying compassion towards animals, the healing and teaching of our fellow human beings together with radiating and displaying love, compassion, mercy and justice in the world.

The successful attainment of psychosynthesis entails us integrating the constituents of our personality, the physical, astral and mental bodies, and its associated qualities and functions, so that it may be infused with the energies of the Higher Self. This is sought with a view to incorporating the energies and qualities of the Soul into our everyday life so that we may then function as its instrument. We are assisted here by the spiritual disciplines of Study of the Ancient Wisdom, the regular practice of Meditation and the performing of spiritual Service work. These serve to increasingly draw the energies of the Higher Self into our aura.

When we tread the spiritual path personality integration is a necessary requirement towards serious spiritual growth. This enables our mind, our emotions and our body to function as one. The personality is 'rounded out' in a manner by which it remains stable under any scenario which it encounters. In this way we are no longer distracted from our spiritual objectives by the transitory affairs of the external world, neither are we bound to it by our emotional attachments and our desires, but rather we operate in conscious co-operation with the Higher Self.

It is important to be aware however, that there are individuals possessing integrated personalities functioning within our contemporary society who are achieving marked levels of success in their pursuit of desire-driven materialistic objectives. This is in accord with what Assagioli described as Self-actualization or Personal Psychosynthesis. This is related to the stage of human evolution where one possesses knowledge of one's personality and control of its various elements. However, such individuals lack a spiritual orientation. This is a prelude to the later stage of divine unrest when such matters begin to lose their appeal as one then experiences the pull of the monad beckoning the return to the source of their being.

If we are to achieve Self-realization, as described by Assagioli, then the various jigsaw components of the personality must be reassembled in such a manner that we are rendered as a worthy recipient of the energies of the Soul. As demonstrated earlier, Psychosynthesis involves a deconstruction of the personality at its present level of consciousness for the purpose of reassembling it at a higher point. This allows the Soul to infuse it with its spiritualising energies.

Evidence of the Soul having satisfactorily quenched its thirst in this respect is in the displayed integration of the personality. Complete integration of personality (i.e., one that is fully infused by the energies of the Soul) is the pinnacle of many lives in which the Soul has harvested the fruits of all experience that life on the planet can offer.

The zodiacal sign which rules spiritual initiation is that of Capricorn. In a manner akin to the mountain goat, when we seek to ascend the cliff-face of the mountain of initiation we will be challenged towards symbolically clinging onto a narrow precipice whilst all around us is crumbling. This may then serve as a vantage point by which we may then ascend further. The sign of Capricorn with its ruling planet Saturn and the 10th house of the natal chart govern patience and endurance, burdens, difficulties, isolation, self-discipline, responsibility and success of an enduring nature. These are hallmarks of the spiritual initiate in the form of the qualities which they demonstrate and the experiences which they have undergone. Capricorn and Saturn also rule synthesis and personality integration which, as we have seen, is a most necessary prelude to us being infused by the energies of the Soul.

Each sign of the zodiac is characterised by a key-phrase. The one associated with Capricorn is that of '*I use*'. Whilst this is especially applicable when Capricorn is placed on the Ascendant in the natal chart, the ability to utilise our various experiences in life, both objective and subjective, towards effecting personality integration as a prelude to being infused by the energies and qualities of the Soul is most important to us all as we tread the path. We should not lose sight of the fact that the Soul incarnates for the purpose of unfolding its latent qualities and therefore chooses appropriate circumstances within which we, as personalities, may develop and grow as an effective instrument towards these ends.

The process of Psychosynthesis therefore requires that we experience what life is offering to us in order to embrace and to integrate the Soul with the personality. The Soul will not wish to leave the Wheel of Rebirth until it has extracted every lesson that life as a human personality can provide. It is important to be aware that the Higher Self has chosen our physical nature, our parents, our family upbringing, our education, our wealth (or lack of it) and so on. We must accept whatever circumstances life presents to us responding to its various challenges with courage, resilience and fortitude. We should remain aware that these experiences present us with opportunities towards our spiritual development and growth.

We must be aware that we are located at the midpoint of two opposite poles (pure spirit and dense matter) and that our objectives should be firmly focussed upon the requirements of the former. Incarnation in matter represents a great challenge to the monad and the attainment of its objective of spiritual staying power. We must be alive to the fact that the pull of matter will exert its effects even when we draw closer to the Soul. These effects can take various forms such as regressive yearnings for material and emotional security. We must remain focussed upon the intent of our spiritual essence and its purpose. Joseph Campbell famously stated that we must render ourselves as *'transparent to transcendence'* whereby the immortal aspect of our being may express its intent.

Central to the endeavours of one treading the path is the accessing of Atma, or divine persistent will. Assagioli emphasised this factor in his work. As well as enabling us to persist in the most challenging circumstances, it is through application of the will that we are able to regulate and direct our psychological processes towards the achievement of Psychosynthesis.

Chapter 20

PSYCHOSYNTHESIS AND THE
BIRTH OF APOLLO AND ARTEMIS

PSYCHOSYNTHESIS IS SYMBOLISED IN CLASSICAL myth by the birth of the Sun god Apollo and his twin, the Moon goddess Artemis. Apollo and Artemis were fathered by Zeus, the king of the Olympian Pantheon of gods, whilst their mother was Leto. Hera, the jealous wife of Zeus, would not allow Leto to give birth on stable land. Hera pursued Leto in relentless fashion until eventually she managed to reach the floating island of Delos despite the strong under-currents surrounding the isle. It was there that she was able to bear her twins. After Leto gave birth, Zeus then secured the island to the bottom of the ocean.

In this myth, Zeus symbolises the divine principle seeking expression in matter. His consort, the jealous Hera, represents the challenges that incarnation in physical form presents to the development and expression of our spirituality. However, the trials and tribulations which we experience here are a necessary part of the evolutionary process in that these enable the monad to attain its objective of acquiring spiritual staying power whereby it may radiate and express its hitherto latent qualities. In achieving this we may perceive the 'secrets of the goddess'. As demonstrated in Chapter 11, these are the secrets of life itself which are only revealed to those who prove themselves worthy by being able to transcend her powers of maya.

We may view Leto as a symbol for the personality seeking to give expression to its innate divine qualities. The floating island of Delos represents the fact that the personality must be fluid and adaptable as a means of enabling the Soul to infuse it with its divine energies. A rigid ego structure is unable to embrace the requirements of Psychosynthesis whereby a deconstruction of the personality at its present level of consciousness occurs for the purpose of reassembling it at a higher point, which then enables one to access the energies of the Higher Self.

Delos is difficult to reach due to strong under-currents. This serves to warn us of the challenges and danger inherent in the process of Psychosynthesis whereby we are subjected to the powerful energies of the unconscious. As demonstrated earlier, these are commonly symbolised as a sea or as an ocean.

It is important to note here that the island of Delos is separated from the mainland. This represents the idea that when treading the path we must seek to extricate ourselves from the conditioning effects of the collective unconscious, located at astro-mental levels, which influences and determines the behavioural patterns of the rank and file of humanity. We are thereby able to access and express the energies and qualities of the archetypal realms of the superconscious which, as we have seen, is located upon the planes of Atma, Buddhi and Manas.[1]

The birth of Apollo represents the coming forth of the solar or spiritual principle from within. Artemis personifies the power of nature and the energies inherent within creation. These include the forces of the unconscious which are symbolised by the forest over which she holds dominion. Artemis is also a chaste goddess representing the requirement for purification of the personality if we

The Birth of Artemis and Apollo by Marcantonio Franceshini

are to gain access to her secrets. This may only occur when we have successfully undertaken the disciplines, and overcome the challenges, of the spiritual path.

Hesiod states that Apollo was born clutching a golden sword. The double-edged nature of the sword is a symbol for the personality which is able to function simultaneously in both the inner and the outer worlds. Douglas Baker would frequently cite the esoteric maxim: '*Not that we should learn to live in this world less but in both worlds more*'. This represents a great challenge, but an essential one, if we are to integrate our mind, emotions and body, together with the associated elements of our character, into a single sovereign entity. As sparks of the divine we are challenged to develop and express our spirituality amidst the constraints of physical form. We must also be aware that we have incarnated as part of a divine plan which entails us functioning as a holistic entity expressing the intent of one in whom we live and move and have our being.

The floating island of Delos being secured to the bottom of the ocean by Zeus symbolises the completion of the process of Psycho-synthesis. The integrated personality is stable amidst the forces of the unconscious, which are represented by the ocean, and is Soul-infused.

In Psychosynthesis the integrated and Soul-infused personality that results from the successful assimilation of our various life experiences, allied to us undertaking spiritual disciplines, is symbolised by the image of the phoenix bird. The phoenix represents the ability of the personality to extricate itself from mundane, materialistic circumstance and to be elevated to a spiritual level of being whereby it is Soul-infused. The phoenix which rises from the ashes of its demise as a self-centred personality then soars towards the Sun, a symbol of its true and immortal nature.

CHAPTER 21

PRACTICES AND CHALLENGES OF THE PATH

WHILST THERE ARE EXISTENTIAL FACTORS AT play when we tread the path, there are various practices or techniques that we can all adopt as a means of assistance. The spiritual path presents us with the challenge towards transmuting the desires of the personality into spiritual aspiration, and overcoming our various habits, impulses, prejudices and complexes as a means of allowing the Soul to infuse us with its energies.

We are advised to undertake the necessary and interrelated practises of Study, Meditation and Service to humanity and/or the planet in general as this enables us to open the symbolic lotus petals of the Soul—Knowledge, Love and Sacrifice—in a balanced and coordinated manner. The practices discussed in this chapter, and others offered throughout this work, may be viewed as complementary to these. All of these serve essentially towards promoting Psychosynthesis. Through us undertaking the spiritual disciplines associated with treading the path, the personality may be tuned to respond to a 'higher octave' whereby it may express the note of the Higher Self as closely as the capabilities of its lower instrument shall allow.

Spiritual service is related to the astrological archetype of Virgo, its planetary ruler the Moon and the 6th house of the natal chart. When Virgo is placed on the Ascendant, the spiritual seeker is advised to adopt the role of the 'spiritual waiter' whereby one performs hard work for the purpose of rendering service to humanity without regard for recognition or thanks. Virgo governs purity and refinement and its presence on the eastern horizon of the chart suggests that 'spiritual cleansing' should be a central theme of one's life whereby one purifies one's attitudes whilst developing a spiritually based system of values. This form of archetypal expression, whilst particularly emphasised when Virgo is placed on the Ascendant of the natal chart, is relevant to us all as we tread the path.

When we seek spiritual transformation it is important to be aware that matters in life which are particularly testing to us can be equally as elevating to the Soul in terms of the realisation of its purpose. Adversity in our lives represents opportunity on our spiritual journey. We are reminded of the famous quote in Shakespeare's *As You Like It*:

> *Sweet are the uses of adversity,*
> *Which, like the toad, ugly and venomous,*
> *Wears yet a precious jewel in his head;*
> *And this our life, exempt from public haunt,*
> *Finds tongues in trees, books in the running brooks,*
> *Sermons in stones, and good in everything*[1]

It is when we experience adverse circumstances in our lives that we are offered the opportunity to express Atma, or divine persistent will, as a means of overcoming these. As I have demonstrated, the Soul incarnates for the purpose of unfolding its latent qualities and towards these ends it chooses appropriate circumstances within which we, as personalities, may develop and grow. We must accept life's various vicissitudes and respond to any of its challenges in an appropriate manner. Challenges serve to test the personality within the crucible of human experience whilst offering the opportunity towards enhancing our spiritual growth.

In a manner akin to the mountaineer who is prepared to persist in the face of inclement circumstances such as freezing cold temperatures and raging blizzards, we must persist in our ascent of the symbolic mountain of spiritual initiation in the knowledge that our efforts are of benefit to humanity itself and to the planetary consciousness as a whole. We should be alive to the opportunities presented to us and be mindful of the fact that spiritual development is achieved by virtue of our efforts, by the purity of our motives and by the causes which we set in motion.

Through the undertaking of spiritual disciplines we seek to align our personal will to that of the Soul. The development and expression of Atma is a most important factor. Our efforts here must include subjecting the personality vehicles to the intent of the Higher Self. This includes the overcoming of our various attachments whether physical, emotional or mental.

In Esoteric Astrology attachments are ruled by the sign of Taurus, its planetary ruler Vulcan and the 2nd house. These factors are indicative of the particular attachments that we are likely to form and which serve as impediments to our spiritual growth if we are unable to overcome these. When Taurus is emphasised in the natal chart, and especially when it is located on the Ascendant, one is often placed in situations where one is required to free oneself as a means of affording greater spiritual expression. Essentially the challenge for Taurus Rising and indeed for us all as we tread the path, is to make the correct use of our material resources and possessions without forming attachments to them. Rather, these should be employed towards evolutionary ends which benefit humanity and the planet as a whole. Taurus rules our values and assets. We should acquire spiritual values and assets whereby our energies are invested in matters eternal as we make deposits in the 'cosmic bank' of the Soul through our expression of its energies.

When we tread the path the physical body and its various impulses, which are instigated primarily by the various drives associated with the astral body, should be trained and harnessed to ensure that these

Sir Galahad by Arthur Hughes

do not lead us towards forms of activity which are inimical to the intent of the Soul. Cleanliness and the use of water, the intake of fresh air, exposure to sunlight allied to a healthy, nutritious diet suited to our constitution are of assistance to us here together with the avoidance of alcohol, tobacco and drugs. It is also worth stating here, however, that when treading the path we are advised not to over-emphasise physical purification at the expense of other more important practices.

The subjecting of the astral body to the will of the Higher Self is of particular importance as we tread the path, and especially the overcoming, transmutation and sublimation of our desire nature. Desire is essentially Atma reflected at the level of the astral plane. We should not allow the energies of our astral body and its associated desires to underlie our endeavours in life whereby we succumb to kama-manas. The regular practice of meditation is of particular assistance to us here in that it serves to discipline the astral body thereby enabling us to exert our control over both its various promptings. This assists us in transmuting the energies of the solar plexus chakra into those of its higher counterpart: the heart chakra.

The control of the mental body is also imperative if we are to attain any serious degree of success in our spiritual endeavours. In accordance with the Hermetic axiom of 'As Above, So Below', just as creation arises from the projected thought of a transcendent being, so we too develop our own mental creations in a similar manner. When treading the path we should seek to create mental images in accord with the intent of the Soul, rather than these simply being incited by kama-manas and by the events of the external world which are conveyed to us by our five senses. It is important to consider the role of an undisciplined imagination in this respect. It is the imagination which enables external objects of desire to exert their power over us. A controlled imagination enables us to lead our thoughts into areas appropriate to our spiritual development and growth rather than allowing an unrestrained imagination to cause us to succumb to the enticements of maya.

On our spiritual journey we, as personalities, should develop a strong sense of empathy for the Soul and the expression of its purpose. We should always be aware that the personality is a transient structure that is adopted and energised by the Soul as a means of its expression. In accordance with an old axiom we should '*learn to love where we are who we are with and what we are doing*'. We should be alive to the opportunities presented to us to develop and express the qualities of the Soul whether these come to us in the guise of privilege or privation. Assagioli states:

'*The Self considers things, events, beings etc., in a very different way to the personal 'I'. Its value system and its perspective is very different to the way the ordinary conscious mind looks at things, with its 'short-sighted views' as Dante put it. What the Self reveals is consistent with what is truly good, but it can be contrary to our wishes or personal preferences.*'[2]

In his work, *The Jewel in the Lotus* Douglas Baker emphasises that Courage, Persistence and Detachment[3] are most essential prerequisites in terms of successfully treading the path. Just as the heroes of myth display great courage when venturing forth into distant and dangerous lands where they are confronted by the tests and trials found therein, we too must demonstrate such heroism and valour as we explore the uncharted realms of our psyche.

Each of the three qualities of Courage, Persistence and Detachment supplement the other two in that they are reflections of Buddhi, Atma and Manas respectively. Cowardice is opposed to courage. We have seen that when treading the path we must accept and face any situation in life which may confront us. Under such circumstances it is most helpful to be aware that the Soul is seeking to test our reliability as its spiritual instrument. We should be mindful of the fact that the Higher Self is also seeking to offload karma which can then free us towards greater acts of spiritual service whilst simultaneously educating us as to the sheer futility of identifying with the transient objects and circumstances of the material world.

Selfishness opposes persistence whereby various forms of self-consideration serve to undermine our ability to persist in our spiritual endeavours. The challenges which we are required to overcome here should be viewed positively as signposts on the path.

Glamour, the allure of that which is transient, is opposed to detachment. We must not allow the veil of maya which envelopes the lower worlds to distract us from our spiritual purpose and neither should it cloud our perspective. When undertaking the inner journey we must cultivate the quality of 'divine indifference' to the fluctuating circumstances of the outer world, to the clamouring of the mind and the emotions, and thereby to identification with the personality, as these are subjected to spiritual disciplines. The allure of transient matters is opposed to such detachment and our ability to discriminate between the real and the unreal. Ephemeral personal considerations must be put aside. Our consciousness is considerably more important than our circumstances.

The Hindu symbol of the swan gracefully floating upon the waters of life without its feathers getting wet is most appropriate as we face our many challenges on the spiritual journey. This is symbolic of the Self-realized individual who maintains a calm and serene manner in the awareness that their spiritual essence is unaffected by any eddies and currents of mundane existence. The swan is also a symbol of one who can ride the symbolic waters of the unconscious in a tranquil manner whilst bathing in the spiritual fire which it reflects thus enabling the expression of the archetypal qualities of the Soul. This process is assisted greatly by the regular practice of meditation which, as demonstrated earlier, serves towards disciplining and controlling the astral body so that we may become free from its various reactions which dictate the course of our thoughts.

The symbol of the swan is related to the planet Jupiter which is the ruler of Aquarius and the 11th house of the natal chart. It is the Aquarian quality of detachment, symbolised by the swan, which we must cultivate if we are to succeed in our spiritual endeavours and particularly so when Aquarius is placed on the Ascendant in the natal chart. We must learn to develop the quality of detachment whereby we maintain an objective view upon various situations in life which we are involved in. This then enables us to operate at the level of the mind rather than that of the emotions avoiding the factor of kama-manas. We may then successfully deal with and obtain psychological and spiritual growth from life's scenarios rather than allowing these to block and/or divert us from expressing the intent of the Soul.

As I have indicated previously, qualities associated with the zodiacal sign of Capricorn provide us with an indication of that which we require if we are to ascend the cliff-face and attain the summit of the symbolic mountain. Patience, endurance and self-discipline are essential pre-requisites here as is the need for us to accept responsibility for all that we do in our lives. This includes the responsibility that we bear in terms of the beneficent or harmful influence which we exert on other people, and upon our environment. We must take responsibility for our own decisions and actions in life and recognising that we, and no one else, are accountable in this respect.

When we tread the path we experience increased responsibilities towards serving humanity. Responsibility brings increased pressure and strain. It is important to be aware here that the factor of stress in our lives provides a mechanism for growth. The analogy employed in Chapter 8, where the immense stress and strain occurring at the tip of a rose bud as it seeks to flower is appropriate here. The opening of the Soul's symbolic lotus petals of knowledge, love and sacrifice occurs in similar fashion.

We must undertake the necessary disciplines and practices associated with the treading of the path in the knowledge that our efforts are not wasted, but rather they are being deposited at the level of the Soul and stored there in its three permanent atoms of Atma, Buddhi and Manas. We may access these qualities, which we have lodged in the 'cosmic bank' of the Soul, both later in this life and in our subsequent incarnations. Our previous lives provide us with potential in that we have created reservoirs here which we can draw upon, these being the energies of Atma, Buddhi and Manas that we have expressed in the past.

CHAPTER 22

THE HEART CHAKRA AND THE
ROLE OF THE WITNESS

IT IS IMPORTANT TO HEED MADAME BLAVATSKY'S well-known statement that when one treads the path all that is good and all that is evil, surface. The emergence of our hard won spiritual talents and gifts from previous lives provide us with ways of expressing the qualities of the Higher Self for the betterment of humanity. These represent a most welcome dividend from the cosmic bank. However, of equal value to us here is the appearance of psychic qualities of a negative nature which enable us to become aware of those aspects of our character which must be eliminated or transmuted so that they no longer impede our spiritual progress. This culminates in the battle between the spiritual disciple and the Dweller on the Threshold which is outlined in the final chapter.

When treading the path we should demonstrate a willing nature towards recognising our faults and any other impediments which inhibit our spiritual expression. We should acknowledge and assess these in a detached manner prior to setting about their removal. It is also worth stating here the dangers of self-deprecation, in the light of discovering our various weaknesses and barriers towards spiritual growth, as this over-emphasises the personality at the expense of the Soul.

One of the techniques related to the practice of Psychosynthesis is to recognise that which is harmful or obstructive in our psyche and that serves towards blocking our spiritual growth, and to then actively cultivate the opposite quality. Therefore, if there is discord and division in our lives we seek to cultivate the quality of harmony; restlessness and impatience must be substituted by a patient, self-disciplined approach; selfish thoughts and attitudes must be replaced by those of an inclusive nature; sensitivity to personal issues must be superseded by sensitivity to the Higher Self and fear supplanted by the expression of courage and so on. By this process negative aspects of our character serve a valuable purpose by making us aware that we must develop their opposite qualities as part of the process of spiritual transformation.

The potency of the astral plane, which gives rise to the factor of desire, is considerably stronger when we are engaged in physical incarnation. As illustrated earlier, when we tread the path a major emphasis is placed upon emotional control and the transmutation and sublimation of desire. The energies of the astral plane are focused upon the solar plexus chakra located in the abdominal region. The astral body synthesises these forces whereby we may use them effectively either towards personal ends, including the pursuit of our various desires, or for the purpose of assisting the evolutionary process by various forms of creative and spiritual expression. The key to achieving the latter is through the transmutation of the energies of the solar plexus chakra into those of the heart chakra, its higher counterpart. The opening of the heart chakra, through the expression of its qualities, is particularly emphasised as we seek spiritual transformation. The Second Ray of Love-Wisdom rules the heart chakra and when treading the spiritual path we place ourselves in the embrace of the mothering ray of our solar system.

Towards these ends we seek to express the qualities of the heart chakra which are related to the buddhic plane whose qualities may be effectively summarised as Love Wisely Applied and Wisdom Lovingly

Applied as previously outlined. We must therefore endeavour to express unconditional and inclusive forms of love as opposed to the selfish or jealous love which is orchestrated by the astral body and the associated energies of the astral plane. It is worth noting here that this does not mean that love of a personal nature should be eliminated, but rather that this is extended to the degree whereby it becomes universal being expressed in altruistic and humanitarian capacities. This represents the transmutation of negative energies related to the 6th Ray of Idealism and Devotion into positive energies related to its higher counterpart, the 2nd Ray of Love-Wisdom.

In our efforts towards transmuting the energies of the solar plexus chakra into those of the heart chakra we should seek to develop a sense of inner peace which arises through the realisation that we are an aspect of the divine life that infuses everything within our universe. This assists us in developing empathy and thereby radiating compassion to other life forms. These interrelated qualities are also associated with the heart chakra. We should endeavour to function as a living centre of peace radiating such energies outwards for the benefit of all. The quality of inner peace also relates to our capacity to obtain inner silence through the regular practice of meditation whereby our thoughts and feelings are quiescent enabling contact between personality and Soul.

We can only truly establish a sense of the peace of eternity in our lives by practising the disciplines of the spiritual path. As we have seen, this leads to Psychosynthesis whereby we are infused by the energies of the Soul. Assagioli writes:

'Peace is only to be found when it is deliberately sought in the higher spiritual world and when a person succeeds in firmly remaining at that level. That sort of peace—far from leading to inertia, to a static tranquillity, or to a passive acceptance—gives new energy. It is a dynamic, creative peace. It is from this place of peace that we direct all our personal activities, provide them with strength, and make them effective and constructive, because they are free from ambition, fear or any sense of attachment, In other words we are able to live as masters, and not as slaves.'[1]

Humility is a quality associated with the heart chakra which is of importance to the spiritual aspirant. When we tread the path there is no need for us to inform, or remind others of our efforts and achievements. As we seek to ascend the symbolic mountain of initiation, an attitude of self-importance only serves as an item of useless baggage which must be set aside if we are to attain the spiritual heights. It is no coincidence that Capricorn, the zodiacal sign governing spiritual initiation, rules the knees which are a symbol of humility. Indeed Capricorn and its planetary ruler Saturn serve to confer humility upon those who lack this quality and, if necessary, metaphorically, if not literally, the archetypal qualities here may force us to our knees in the process. Spiritual initiation will not occur unless we are prepared to metaphorically kneel as a means of receiving the energies transmitted by the initiatory rod.

The practice of harmlessness is required if we are to successfully tread the path. We should seek to practice harmlessness in our thoughts, in our speech and in our actions. The requirement for us to cultivate the quality of harmlessness is based upon the realisation that all forms are aspects of the one divine life and therefore to emit any sort of harmful energy only serves to harm both the sender and the recipient. The true practice of harmlessness prevents us from creating difficult karma as we are confronted by life's challenges whilst it also serves to promote right human relations.

The importance of expressing courage was outlined in the previous chapter. This is also a heart chakra quality. When we tread the path we must display courage in facing whatever situations confront us in life in the knowledge that these are relevant to our spiritual growth as the Soul tests our worthiness as its instrument of expression whilst accelerating the offloading of karma. In displaying courage, as symbolised by the heroes of myth, we overcome fear, this being located in the solar plexus chakra.

As I have previously indicated, the heart chakra quality of discrimination is important also. This relates to our ability to discriminate between that which is spiritual and that which is of a merely transient nature, as a means of becoming free from the maya of the lower worlds. The Hindus refer to this as 'viveka'. In his celebrated work, *Vivekachudamani*, Shankara describes the faculty of discrimination as the 'crown jewel' amongst the essential qualities required for us to obtain. We must seek to perceive the underlying reality or noumenon behind each and every phenomenon. By doing so our powers of human reason are neither obscured nor diverted by our passions and personal feelings, but rather we are able to pursue a direction in our lives which is in accord with the intent of the Soul.

As a means of achieving this, it can assist us greatly if we create a division within ourselves consisting of the Doer or the Observed and the Witness or the Observer. When we adopt the role of the observer we exercise self-remembrance whereby we are able to choose the manner in which we react to circumstances and events in our lives, rather than responding in a mechanical fashion. When we become aware of the impressions which such circumstances and events create within us, we may then react in a conscious rather than an unconscious manner as we develop insight and understanding into the dynamics and predispositions of our personality, and particularly the astral and mental bodies.

There is a well-known and valuable Dis-identification Exercise which can assist us greatly towards adopting the role of the observer. Assagioli writes:

> '*Drives and desires constitute the active, dynamic aspect of our psychological life. The procedure necessitates disidentification from them, at least temporarily, and this in turn means acquiring awareness of the self, the conscious "I", as distinct from these psychological elements and forces, and from that central point of observing their flow.*'[2]

We begin the exercise by relaxing our bodies and whilst affirming that we possess a physical body, we recognise this as our instrument or vehicle. We state here: '*I am not my body, I am the knower of my body*'.

We then proceed to observe our astral body and our recent, or current, emotional state of being. Again we affirm that, whilst we are experiencing the emotional content of our psyche, we are not these transient fleeting, emotions of an oscillatory nature. We affirm: '*I am not my emotions, I am the knower of my emotions*'.

Finally, we observe the activity of our mind or mental body. Again we affirm that we possess a mind whilst recognising that its ceaselessly changing content does not constitute our real and enduring nature. Here we declare: 'I am not my thoughts, I am the knower of my thoughts'.

We may then ask ourselves the question, '*Who Am I?*' as a means of asserting the independence and the authority of the Soul. We may answer this question by affirming to ourselves: '*I am a being of light, I am a centre of pure consciousness, love and will*'.

The regular practice of this exercise enables us to pass through each stage of dis-identification in a swift and dynamic manner. We may then remain in the 'I' consciousness for as long as we require. We are thus able to dis-identify from any overwhelming emotion or irritating thought by adopting the attitude of the observer. This offers us insight into the meaning and causes of the situation together with the most effective means of addressing it.

The human personality is partly constituted by what exponents of psychosynthesis refer to as 'sub-personalities'. These may be described as functions or aspects of an individual who lacks psychological integration. Sub-personalities are primarily personality structures which we have developed as a means of coping with the circumstances that we have previously encountered in infancy, childhood, adolescence and early adulthood.

Through observing our actions and reactions to the various scenarios which we encounter in life, and by analysing the motivating factors which function here, we quickly become aware of our various sub-personalities which assume centre stage depending upon the dictates of our social circumstances. These fragments of our overall personality take many forms. These little 'I's' serve to divert our attention from the real and enduring aspect of our being. It can be helpful to identify our sub-personalities by labelling these. Common sub-personalities include the protector/controller; the critic; the perfectionist; the mother; the father; the organiser; the victim; the bully; the idealist, to name but a few. The adoption and expression by humanity of these 'archetypal roles' is related to their respective morphic fields which we considered in Chapter 12.

When we become aware of these often disparate aspects of ourselves, and when we practice discrimination, we begin to emphasise and assert both the authority and the independence of the Higher Self. Such awareness enables us to recognise and accept our sub-personalities so that they may be transformed into a higher unity rather than us merely responding to their dictates. On this subject Douglas Baker observes:

'In order to have a genuine synthesis, there has to be a higher order centre around which the synthesis can occur. The higher order synthesis becomes the integrated personality. Before this integration, not only can we be limited by a particular sub-personality, but also by the conflicts that arise between two or more of them. Sometimes, the unity of selves occurs around another little "I", such as the child in us. If this occurs, this kind of integration can force us to live our whole life in that role… that of dependence on another. The breaking up of this kind of integration produces suffering because it is breaking up an old pattern, but the outcome is growth and maturation.'[3]

The sounding of the question, *'Who Am I?'* is of value to us here also as it serves towards bringing the personality and its associated drives and sub-personalities into check, thus assisting towards our functioning as an instrument of the Soul. We may ask ourselves this question as often as we deem it necessary to assert the authority of the Higher Self.

Another valuable technique towards promoting Psychosynthesis is that of the 'evening review'. This exercise is best practised just prior to sleep. When lying in bed, after relaxing the body and stilling the emotions and mind, we review the content of the preceding day in a backward sequence. We commence with our current situation then reverse to late evening, to early evening to late afternoon, and so on until our awakening in the morning. Whilst conducting the evening review we should adopt an objective, detached and non-critical perspective. The experiences here are not to be relived but rather we seek to extract their meaning. This enables us both to deal more effectively with the Dweller on the Threshold whilst also being a valuable method for observing and dealing with our various sub-personalities.

The reversal of the sequence of time here serves a twofold purpose. Firstly, it lessens the tendency of the mind to follow its standard linear thought mode of past, present and future. This is important as the realms of higher consciousness do not obey the laws of time and space which are related to our physical world. Secondly, by following a backward route here, we find it easier to observe the underlying causes which determine our conduct and actions.

CHAPTER 23

THE HERCULES MYTH AND THE DWELLER ON THE THRESHOLD

As illustrated throughout this work, the symbolism found within the hero myths of our world illustrates the great challenges which confront us as we tread the spiritual path. It is by successfully negotiating such challenges that we are able to prove our worthiness towards proceeding further so that ultimately we may obtain our goal.

One of the most fundamental challenges in treading the path is to subjugate the personality, and all that is associated with its functioning, to the intent of the Soul. This is a subjective event. We have seen previously that the subterranean levels of the human psyche are commonly symbolised by the cave, both in dream imagery and in myth. This relates to matters which are located at deep or hidden levels of our being and therefore concealed to the outer world. In the symbolic representation of the personality being harnessed to the intent of the Soul, the symbolism of the cave plays an important and necessary role. Cave symbolism is found in the Twelve Labours of Hercules which, as I stated in the chapter one, represent the challenges and the potential spiritual gifts, presented to the Soul by incarnation in the twelve signs of the zodiac as it journeys through these for the last time upon the Cardinal Cross. It is upon the Cardinal Cross that the personality is subjected to the will of the Soul as a means of unfolding its symbolic sacrifice petals and ultimately obtaining liberation from the Wheel of Rebirth.

In common with many of the heroes of myth, Hercules possesses dual parentage in the form of a divine father, Zeus, and an earthly mother, Alcmene. This represents the essential duality of humanity in that we possess both a spiritual and a material aspect to our being.

In her book, *The Labours of Hercules,* Alice Bailey assigns the Herculean labour of The Slaying of the Nemean Lion to the astrological sign of Leo. In esoteric astrology this zodiacal sign, together with its planetary ruler—the Sun, and the 5th house of the natal chart, governs the personality and also our capacity towards obtaining wholeness of being whereby the conscious and unconscious components of our psyche function in unison. The attainment of this enables us to function in a manner akin to a miniature Sun. We are then able to radiate spiritual energies outwards, and especially those of the heart chakra, which also comes under the astrological domain of Leo, for the purpose of sustaining and illuminating those who are 'constellated' around us.

In this labour Hercules is required to overcome a lion which has been devastating the land and terrorising its inhabitants. The Nemean Lion symbolises a powerful integrated personality lacking in the necessary spiritual orientation. The lion runs wild leaving a trail of havoc in its wake. At the present juncture of human evolution there are many individuals in our world who function in this manner.

Hercules followed the lion up a narrow mountain path and into a cave. He entered the cave only to find that the lion had left by a second opening. He then gathered some wood and sticks and piled them together to block one of the two openings to the cave before chasing the lion into the cave through the unblocked entrance. Hercules then discarded his trusted club and choked the lion with his bare hands.

Bailey reveals a profound symbolism relating to the two entrances to the cave. The pituitary gland, which is related to the ajna or brow chakra, is housed in a cave-like structure within the head. The post-pituitary lobe is associated with personal emotions and the anterior pituitary with spiritual qualities. Hercules was required to close the former for the purpose of controlling the personality by means of the higher mind. He was required to subdue the lion of personality within the cave by entering though the opening of the higher mind. By blocking the opening related to personal emotions, and by discarding his club, Hercules refuses to lead a life driven by kama-manas, preferring to overcome his various desires for the purpose of aligning himself to the purpose of the Soul.

The symbolism here indicates that the subordination of the personality to the intent of the Soul takes place within the subjective realms of the human psyche. The tests and trials which we are faced with in this respect culminate in the battle between the spiritual disciple and The Dweller on the Threshold. This term was first used by the English mystic Edward Bulwer Lytton in his novel *Zanoni*. The anthroposophical teachings of Rudolf Steiner refer to the Dweller as the Guardian of the Threshold. The Dweller may be described as the sum total of our lower nature whose effects have been created over our many lives. This is the aggregation of our fears, our subdued passions, and also all of the repressed and undesirable aspects of our character. When we seek to scale the symbolic mountain of initiation we must confront and deal with the Dweller.

The Dweller is an entity that blocks or guards the threshold of initiation into higher states of consciousness. It is only upon the spiritual disciple attaining the third initiation that the Dweller ceases to exist and is replaced by the Angel of the Presence. As stated previously, this is the devic or angelic aspect of the Causal Body, the Temple of the Soul. The Angel of the Presence, or Solar Angel, guards the portal of initiation deciding the eligibility of the ego to receive inflows of ideas of divine origin which reflect spiritual attributes from qualities gained in our past lives. These emanate from the planes of Atma, Buddhi and Manas and represent the true source of genius and of inspiration.

Cerberus by William Blake

On this subject Bailey writes:

> *'The Dweller on the Threshold does not emerge out of the fog of illusion and glamour until the disciple is nearing the Gates of Life. Only when we catch dim glimpses of the Portal of Initiation and an occasional flash of light from the Angel of the Presence Who stands waiting beside that door, can he come to grips with the principle of 'duality', which is embodied for him in the Dweller and the Angel.'* [1]

We deal with the Dweller by confronting it and recognising it for what it actually is. To achieve this we are required to focus and concentrate our energies on the Higher Self and its objectives thereby weakening and dissipating the Dweller by causing its energy supply to cease. However, we must be aware that the Dweller will fight back and will seek to highlight negative and challenging situations in our life as a means of reasserting its authority. It is therefore a very challenging task to dispel the Dweller and reveal the Angel of the Presence through bringing the qualities of Atma, Buddhi and Manas into our aura. On this matter, Douglas Baker writes:

'Memories of this life and indeed previous ones surface and these together form the Dweller. The Dweller is a loathsome entity being comprised of astral matter of the lowest order. It preys on the neophyte drawing its substance from them during times of fear, horror, worry and any other form of negative thinking during which the not-yet integrated astral body haemorrhages. The Dweller forms a negative vortex of a force field of which the chela is the positive and donating pole. The Dweller is dispatched when it is deliberately confronted and recognised for what it is. The flow of auric energies to the Dweller is then strangulated whereby it flags and withers. But it will take every opportunity to fight back for its survival seeking to highlight any negative scene or emotion and usually where the disciple is shifting their focus from the outer world to the inner. It is finally replaced with the birth and the steady growth of the 'Angel of the Shining Presence' representing structures in Atma, Buddhi and Manas which are steadily being built into the aura through the assiduous efforts of the disciple in meditation and through his service to mankind and his devotion to the study of the occult classics...'[2]

In esoteric astrology the Dweller is represented by the sign of Scorpio, its planetary ruler Mars, and the 8th house of the natal chart. This astrological archetype provides the opportunity to overcome obstacles that impede further spiritual growth and associated expansions of consciousness by enabling us to invoke the hero archetype. The tests and trials which we encounter here should be viewed as opportunities for spiritual growth and regeneration as they lead to ultimate victory in terms of the Soul's evolutionary growth. The presence of the Dweller, and one's impending battle with it, is particularly emphasised when Scorpio is placed on the Ascendant in the natal chart.

Whilst the archetypal energies of Scorpio present the individual on the path with great challenges they also bestows the necessary courage and heroism for the purpose of one both coping and flourishing under such circumstances. If utilised correctly, obstacles and setbacks in our life can induce rapid spiritual growth. The aforementioned Shakespearean quote, *'Sweet are the uses of adversity*' is particularly applicable to the challenges engendered by the Scorpio archetype which entails the expression of heroic qualities. Probably the most famous, and most challenging of the Herculean labours is assigned to incarnation in the sign of Scorpio: Destroying the Lernaen Hydra. Hercules is instructed to destroy a nine-headed hydra that dwells by a festering swamp beside a river. He is advised that one of the hydra's heads is immortal and that if any of the hydra's heads is destroyed then another two would grow in its place.

To entice the hydra from its lair Hercules dips his arrows in burning pitch then fires them into the cavern where it dwells. The hydra emerges standing three fathoms high with its nine heads breathing fire. It appears to have been created from the foulest thoughts which humanity could conceive of. When Hercules destroys one of the heads of the monster, two then emerge. The hydra seems to increase in strength after each attack. Hercules then sinks to his knees grasping the hydra with his bare hands and holding it aloft. The monster which was invincible in the darkness, mud and slime lost its power and withered in the sunlight. As it lay on the ground, Hercules observed the immortal head of the monster which he cut off and buried under a rock.

The hydra may be held to symbolise the Dweller and our lower nature in general. The dark swamp where the hydra resides represents the subterranean regions of the human psyche located at the lower levels, or sub-planes, of the astral plane. This is where the primal instincts, passions, lusts and desires of humanity are located. If we are susceptible to these then we are faced with the danger of metaphorically 'drowning' in the lower realms of the unconscious. The capacity of the hydra to grow two heads, in response to one of its heads being destroyed, is symbolic of the esoteric fact that we cannot repress various aspects of our lower nature as the longer we do this the more potent is the backlash which we must later face. Rather, these must be confronted and thereafter transmuted as an important part of the process of spiritual transformation.

The Dweller utilises the collective phobias, idiosyncrasies and thought-forms of humanity by virtue of their associated morphic fields. It draws upon these as a means of reasserting its dominion.

When we are able to destroy our individual dweller we also perform an act of service on behalf of humanity in that we lessen the influence of humanity's dweller, by reducing the potency of its morphic field which is anchored to the lower planes of the astral world.

The battle with the Dweller is symbolised in the confrontation between Hercules and the hydra and in the other Herculean labour which we shall consider shortly: The Slaying of Cerberus. As I demonstrated previously, this is paralleled by the challenge which confronted Theseus whereby he was required to enter the maze, a symbol of the labyrinthine astro-mental realms of the psyche and their illusionary qualities, as a means of overcoming the half-man, half-beast Minotaur. The Minotaur blocked his entry to the centre of the maze, which symbolises the Soul, as the instrument of the monad.

It is only when we release our arrows of spiritual aspiration that the presence of the Dweller is revealed. When treading the path, like Hercules, we must apply discrimination to recognise its presence, search patiently and then destroy that which we encounter. This requires great courage and strength. Whilst Hercules fought in the swamp amidst the mud and slime he could not conquer the hydra. Similarly, we cannot overcome our lower nature by confronting it on its own level. However, when we move the problem to a higher spiritual dimension the light and wisdom of the Soul is too much for the Dweller, and other aspects of our lower nature, to withstand.

In the classical teachings, this labour relates to the second initiation when the Soul-orientated personality is able to discipline, control and transmute the various desires of the personality towards spiritual ends. This is followed by the third initiation when the Dweller is finally dispatched.

The desire nature is particularly expressed through the sacral chakra in the form of sexual expression, and the solar plexus chakra in the form of selfish or jealous love. The energy here must be transmuted into spiritual qualities through the throat and heart centres where true creativity and unconditional love are expressed respectively. A key to this process is that of achieving mental polarisation whereby we must be centred at the level of the mind rather than that of the emotions thereby avoiding kama-manas. Without mental polarisation focus upon serious spiritual development is futile as our endeavours are merely imposed and driven by maya. It is worth noting that one of the hydra's heads was immortal and that Hercules buried it under a rock indicating that despite the ability of the hero to overcome it in battle, the Dweller and the forces of the lower astral plane, together with our shadow characteristics, remain present and that it is by subjecting these to the force of our will, by purifying the vibrations of our various bodies and not engaging in any thoughts driven by these levels of being that we remain free from their influence.

The Herculean labour where the Dweller is finally dispatched and which Bailey relates to the third initiation is symbolised by The Slaying of Cerberus. She assigns this labour to Capricorn, the zodiacal sign which rules spiritual initiation. Hercules is required to rescue Prometheus who has defied the gods by stealing their fire which enables the progression and civilisation of humanity. The supreme Olympian deity Zeus punished the transgression of Prometheus by assigning him to the kingdom of Hades where a vulture pecked at his liver. Prometheus may be viewed here as a symbol for humanity itself. The vulture pecking at his liver is representative of the five senses. This symbolises the painful and debilitating effects which the five senses exert upon us if we are unable to overcome the effects of kama-manas. This emphasises the importance of meditation whereby we shut down the five senses as a means of connecting with the Higher Self.

The underworld is a symbol for the unconscious and therefore the subjective realms of the human psyche. It is here where the archetypal process of spiritual transformation occurs whereby the desire nature is overcome and the five senses no longer serve to engage us in the pursuit of transient forms of satisfaction, but rather we operate within the physical world in accordance with the intent of the Soul. As we have seen, Jung's concept of Individuation entails the unification of the conscious and unconscious elements of the psyche so that we may function in accordance with the intent of what he described as the 'Self'.

After treading many labyrinthine paths Hercules arrives at the court of Hades who asks him what he, a living mortal, seeks in his realms. Hercules states that he wishes to free Prometheus from his burden. Hades advises him that the path to Prometheus is guarded by a monstrous three-headed dog called Cerberus and that if he can overcome the creature then he could unbind the tortured hero.

Cerberus is another symbol for the Dweller. Hercules confronts Cerberus and by tightly grasping the central head, despite the dog's demonic fury, he conquers it. This symbolises the overcoming of the Dweller when it is deliberately confronted and recognised for what it actually is. This enabled Hercules to then free Prometheus. The act of freeing the suffering hero is symbolic of the spiritual aspirant by overcoming the Dweller thereby being eligible to receive the fiery energies of spiritual initiation where an alignment occurs between the monad and its instrument of expression, the Soul, as the Angel of the Presence is revealed.

THE SPIRITUAL DIARY

The spiritual diary is one of the most important tools available to us as we tread the spiritual path. It is important that we begin to record elements of our subjective life and the diary provides us with the means for doing so. The setting up and maintaining of the spiritual diary provides a systematic method for recording matters that are relevant to the Soul, its development and the expression of its purpose: dreams, visions, impressions, progress with meditation, service work, esoteric studies and even changes in the physical body. The diary ultimately becomes a link between us and the Higher Self, serving as the mechanism by which we may seek counsel from the Higher Self and, if set up properly, provide us with an invaluable record of direct inner response.

How To Set Up The Diary

Select a hard bound book (*not* a calendar diary). The diary must then be personalised and dedicated, stating the purpose for which it will be used. Excerpts from classical occult literature should be entered regularly, i.e. *The Voice of the Silence* by H.P. Blavatsky, *Light On the Path* by Mabel Collins, *At the Feet of the Master* by Krishnamurti or any other classical literature or poetry which elicits a response from within and attunes to disciple to the qualities of the Higher Self. This helps to set the tone of reverence. A persistent record should be made of dreams, meditations, service work, revelations etc.

The Purpose of The Diary

The following is taken from the content of the Claregate audio-visual, online correspondence course. Foundations in Esoteric Studies which, in turn, was adapted from the earlier Claregate Correspondence Course. The spiritual diary is a record of one's spiritual effort, struggles and achievements and is concerned with matters which help implement the Soul's Purpose. It serves as a valuable chronology of our progress along the path. If maintained conscientiously, it will provide essential guidance in times of stress or great difficulties, demonstrating to us that the Soul is ever on watch and guiding its personality vehicle. The spiritual diary is a mechanism for bringing into full consciousness elements of the psyche. The diary lays down a channel for the transmission of advice and direction from the Higher Self that can bring about a transformation of the personality, its attachments and limitations. It calls forth, in the most evocative manner, such Soul-baring confessions of the neophyte as to provide a catalyst for the removal of those personality blocks which keep the 'Voice of the Silence' from becoming an articulate and immanent consultant.

It sets the tone and the pace for the personality expression until these become integrated into one's nature and no longer need a spur. The philosophical way of life becomes a reality. It is a way that is undisturbed by the breezes of competitive living and the eddies and currents of insecurity and fear. An effectively maintained spiritual diary leads the weary traveller to the fountains of their being, brainwashes the personality to the dictates of its Soul—producing a conversion back to a path from which the disciple has been straying the moment from birth. The secret here is that a re-orientation to the Soul, rather than the personality, is achieved.

The inner springs are stimulated to release their high content of memories garnered from previous lives. A rapport is set up between these elements of the collective superconscious, the psyche and the permanent atoms of the lower triad which in some establishes the foundations for genius. Together these impulses give new impetus to the personality. In psychoanalysis the individual is freed from the childhood psyche. In discipleship one must be freed from the Dweller on the Threshold- the sum total of all the deposits of personality experiences in this and earlier lives which includes one's personal share of the collective unconscious of humanity. The diary prepares the disciple for confrontation with the Dweller evoking pointers from the Soul as to which elements of the Dweller must be faced next.

The diary is intended to highlight those difficulties which arise from the adjustments which the disciple must make in the outer world if they are to live the philosophical and meditative way of life. When a question is posited in the diary the Higher Self can make suggestions through meditation and the dream life as to how these adjustments can be effected.

The spiritual diary is not intended to help the disciple to escape painful episodes in life but rather to demonstrate that pain is related to the impermanence of matter. All relationships based on a form structure will ultimately pass away.

Mystical experience is a joy in itself but when it rewards the endeavours of a spiritually-oriented personality it transcends all others because it adds *meaning* to the life. Many disciples say that they can withstand suffering as long as there is meaning to it. The diary coordinates the world of action with the world of causes thus providing insight into the factor of karma.

The spiritual diary must be poised ever ready to analyse, assess and evaluate every motive. The search for the signposts of real spiritual growth is fostered by the diarist who must ever be sincere with themselves. Writing untruths in one's spiritual diary is like cheating at patience.

GLOSSARY

Adept one who has undergone the five major initiations, as described in the wisdom teachings. At the fifth initiation consciousness is transferred from the human kingdom to the Fifth Kingdom of Souls.

Angel of the Presence also sometimes referred to as 'The Angel of the Shining Presence' or 'Solar Angel'. This is the devic or angelic aspect of the causal body. This term often refers to the presence and awareness of the Soul after the spiritual aspirant has successfully overcome the Dweller on the Threshold and attained the Third Initiation (see Dweller on the Threshold).

Antakarana also referred to as the Rainbow Bridge. The Antakarana is the bridge between the Soul or Higher Self and the personality. The antakarana links the higher and lower mind and is constructed through the practice of abstract thought which relates to the three highest sub-planes of the mental plane. Meditation is a particularly effective way towards strengthening and widening the Antakarana where the Soul responds to the efforts of the personality here by passing down energy and meaning via this bridgehead. The Antakarana is also constructed through study of the Ancient Wisdom and through spiritual service work

Anu the building blocks of matter on each of the seven planes of consciousness and residing on each respective highest subplane. Combinations of anu give rise to the substance of nature's various planes. The anu is essentially an indivisible energy vortex. Anu or ultimate atoms receive, transmit and transmute the energy from higher to lower planes. On the physical plane the anu is a sub-atomic particle found within a quark. Science has yet to locate the anu although it does possess a Superstring Theory which proposes that quarks are comprised of tiny strings which vary in length between ten to thirty five metres.

Archetypes energy reservoirs found within what Jung referred to as the 'Collective Unconscious'. Archetypes may be described as 'divine ideas which arise from the energies and the interactions of the Seven Rays. They are first expressed on the spiritual planes of consciousness where the Soul resides—those of Atma, Buddhi and Higher Manas. These regions are referred to by Roberto Assagioli and Douglas Baker as the 'superconscious'. Archetypes enter the human aura through the chakras and are generally expressed through the chakras above the diaphragm. The archetypes have also been elaborated by humanity's history—all our thoughts and feelings, our comprehensions, our struggles, our experiences of happiness and beauty and so on are deposited into these giant reservoirs which exist within the precincts of our planet.

Astral Body comprised of the substance of the astral plane, the astral body, together with the mental and physical bodies, is part of the personality. The astral and mental bodies are comprised of the elemental life, referred to as elemental essence, found within their respective planes. Spiritual growth, and its associated expansions of consciousness, occurs through the practice of various spiritual disciplines (such as study, meditation, service to humanity, discrimination, compassion, detachment) which bring these bodies under control so that matter of a finer and higher vibratory nature which is more responsive to the qualities of the Soul or Higher Self can be brought into these bodies from their respective planes. This leads to personality integration whereby the personality can operate as an effective instrument of the Soul whereby it is not distracted from its purpose by the ephemeral and the transient.

Atlantis this is the continent where the fourth Root Race evolved. The purpose of the Atlantean Root Race was to develop and open the solar plexus chakra

Atma the Soul is comprised of the qualities of atma, buddhi and higher manas. Atma may be described as 'divine persistent will' which relates to the ability to maintain one's spiritual focus and endeavours regardless of whatever circumstances in life may confront them. Atma is expressed most effectively and harmoniously through the physical body.

Buddhi the Soul is comprised of the qualities of atma, buddhi and higher manas. The quality of Buddhi relates to love wisely applied and wisdom lovingly applied, intuition, inclusiveness and compassion. Buddhi is expressed most effectively and harmoniously through the astral body.

Causal Body the name Causal body is derived from the fact that within it reside the causes which manifest as effects on the planes below it. The Causal body acts as a vehicle for the Soul whilst also storing the essence of one's spiritual expression throughout thier physical incarnations. The Causal body consists of the substance of the first three mental subplanes and is dissipated at the fourth initiation.

Collective Unconscious Jung referred to the collective unconscious as containing both archetypes and instinctual patterns of human behaviour. The wisdom teachings acknowledge that the collective and our personal unconscious represent a storehouse of instinctual forces whilst also postulating a super-conscious from which the archetypes emanate. This is located at the levels which the wisdom teachings refer to as Atma, Buddhi and Higher Manas- the realms of the Higher Self.

Devas the word 'deva' is derived from Sanskrit and translates as 'shining ones'. The deva evolution runs parallel to the human. As the creation process unfolds various ranks of devas come forth one from within another. Devas are responsible for the construction of all levels of creation and the various forms found therein. The deva evolution is hierarchical in structure from archangels down to the tiny nature spirits of folklore.

Devachan the true heaven state where the Soul rests between incarnations. The presence of universal joy and bliss pervade here with the extent of these being determined by the spiritual qualities which have been earned through their previous incarnations.

Dweller on the Threshold the sum total of our lower nature of which the effects have been created over our previous lives. The Dweller on the Threshold is the aggregation of our fears, and the repressed and undesirable aspects of our character. When the Dweller is dispatched by the spiritual aspirant at the Third Initiation it is replaced by the Angel of the Presence which is a representation of the Soul or Higher Self.

Egoic Lotus term depicting the Soul as a three-tiered lotus structure comprised of petals of knowledge, love and sacrifice, At the end of our evolutionary sojourn when liberation from the Wheel of Rebirth is achieved the three central petals are opened to reveal the Jewel in the Lotus,

Etheric Body comprised of the substance of the four highest physical sub-planes, this sub-atomic structure energises and vitalises the dense physical body through the agency of prana.

Fifth Kingdom this is the realm of the Soul or Higher Self. The other kingdoms in nature are:1. the mineral kingdom; 2. the plant or vegetable kingdom; 3. the animal kingdom; 4. the human kingdom.

Fire see Chapter Four Notes.

Higher Manas the Soul is comprised of the qualities of atma, buddhi and higher manas. Higher manas relates to the practice of abstract thought- thought abstracted from the constraints of the physical and astral worlds and therefore from our senses and our desires. Abstract thought is developed through study of the arts, philosophy, esoteric writings and especially through studying and interpreting the symbolism found in myth and the imagery associated with dreams and meditations. The practice of abstract thought serves to construct the antakarana or rainbow bridge which links the personality to the Soul and enables the Soul to increasingly flood the personality with its energies (see also, antakarana, astral body and higher manas). Higher manas is expressed most effectively and harmoniously through the mental body.

Higher Triad the permanent atoms of the Soul residing on the plane of atma, buddhi and manas.

Hylozoism this word describes the principle that all forms are filled with life from the tiniest atom to the greatest galaxy. All forms provide vehicles through which aspects of the divine life, at varying stages of a long evolutionary journey, may develop and express their latent qualities.

Hypnogogia the state of awareness just before sleep (also see Hypnopompia). Hypnopompia- the state of awareness as one comes out of the sleep state.

Individuation this a term originated by Carl Jung of which the goal is that of 'wholeness' or 'integration' which describes the unification of the conscious and unconscious aspects of the human psyche

Initiation the process of initiation applies two factors to the individual concerned- a tremendous increase in one's awareness and a considerably greater capacity towards carrying the life force. In classical esoteric teachings there are five major initiations (described here under Notes for Chapter One) which occur during our long evolutionary sojourn towards unfolding the flower of the Soul. When the fifth initiation is reached one is then described as a Master or Adept.

Karma this relates to the law of cause and effect where every action possesses a corresponding reaction. It is only when we are entirely 'Soul-infused' that we no longer produce karma in the lower worlds of existence, the realms of the personality.

Lemuria refers to the continent of the Third Root Race- the Lemurian. It was on Lemuria that humanity first occupied physical bodies on this planet. The purpose of the Lemurian Root Race was to develop and open the sacral chakra. Lower Triad- the permanent atoms from which the personality bodies are derived- physical, astral and mental.

Manas see Higher manas.

Maya the concept of maya refers to that which is transient and therefore 'non-enduring'. It is the Soul or Higher Self is therefore the 'Real' and enduring aspect of our nature whilst the mental, astral and physical bodies, together with the worlds which they are inhabit, are held to be illusory or mayavic. Maya results from our own preconceptions and imperfections which prevent us from apprehending the 'Real' or inner nature of that which we perceive.

Mental Body comprised of the substance of the mental plane. The mental body, together with the astral and physical bodies, is part of the personality. The astral and mental bodies are comprised of the elemental life, referred to as elemental essence, found within their respective planes. Unlike the other personality bodies, the mental body is only half-formed. It is comprised of the substance of the four lower sub-planes of the mental plane. It is through the practice of abstract thought or higher manas (see also higher manas) that the spiritual aspirant constructs the antakarana or rainbow bridge which links the personality to the Soul and enables the Soul to increasingly flood the personality with its energies (see also, antakarana, astral body and higher manas).

Monad this is our spiritual essence. Classical esoteric teachings inform us that we are indivisible sparks of a divine flame referred to as The One Flame Divine or Solar Logos. To assist in the evolution of the Solar Logos projects its component parts downward into the lower planes of matter for the purpose of developing its latent qualities by gaining experience of the planes of consciousness below it which are converted into faculties and to gain 'spiritual staying power'. Due to its purity of vibration the monad itself cannot descend beyond its own plane of existence so it adopts mechanisms which can operate at these lower levels of consciousness. The Soul, which is a reflection of the monad, serves as its instrument of expression on the planes of atma, buddhi and higher manas and the personality serves as the instrument of the Soul on the lower mental, astral and physical planes.

Permanent Atoms with the cooperation of deva forces the monad appropriates atoms on the planes of atma, buddhi, manas, the lower mental, astral and physical planes. These are retained by the monad throughout the entire period of manifestation. These serve as force centres which store consciousness, memory and the faculties derived from one's expression of the energies of their respective planes throughout all incarnations. The mental, astral and physical permanent atoms also determine the sheaths of their respective personality bodies.

Personality the personality is comprised of its physical, astral and mental bodies and serves as the instrument of the Soul or Higher Self on these respective planes of consciousness. Spiritual growth occurs through the personality expressing the qualities of the Soul (see atma, buddhi and higher manas) whilst in physical incarnation.

Personality Integration refers to a personality where the physical, astral and mental bodies are stable and blended. Such a personality is independent and completely self-sufficient being free from any emotional attachments whilst holding no fixed attitudes or ideas. The Soul may then infuse the personality with its energies to maximum effect.

Prana this is the vital force which sustains and vitalises the physical body. It is taken into the human body primarily through the act of breathing. Prana is attached to oxygen molecules. It flows through the subtle filaments within the etheric body known as nadis which underlie the nervous system thereby vitalising and energising the physical body.

Psychopomp the psychopomp is the aspect of the Soul which seeks to unite the personality with its purpose and intent. The word psychopomp is derived from the Greek language, literally meaning 'guide of souls'. The psychopomp relates the unconscious realms of the human psyche to those of a conscious nature.In its role as a divine messenger the psychopomp functions primarily through the medium of symbol occurring mainly through dreams, meditation and synchronicities

Psychosynthesis term originated by Roberto Assagioli which describes the process of creating an integrated personality which is infused with the energies of the Soul (see personality integration).

Root Race/Sub Race each life-wave of manifestation on our planetary globe is known as a world period and is divided into seven stages which are referred to as Root Races. These are also divided into seven stages known as sub-races. The 5th Root Race known as the Aryan is the one currently evolving on our planet and its purpose is to develop the throat chakra. This was preceded by the 4th Root Race- the Atlantean which in turn was preceded by Lemurian or Third Root Race when humanity first took on physical form on this planet. The first and second Root Races were non-physical (see also Atlantis and Lemuria).

Samadhi a state of superconscious experience achieved through meditation

Seven Rays the seven streams of divine force whose output activates, constructs and maintains our solar system. The Seven Rays are:
Rays of Aspect
  1. Will and Power
  2. Love-Wisdom
  3. Active Intelligence
Rays of Attribute
  4. Art and Harmony Thru Conflict
  5. Concrete Knowledge and Science
  6. Idealism-Devotion
  7. Ceremonial Order and Ritual

Soul/Higher Self the immortal and enduring part of our nature which serves as the instrument of the monad and which exists for the purpose of obtaining a complete from of consciousness where it is responsive to every vibration of life surrounding it on each and every level of existence. This requires control of the energies and forces on the various planes of existence. The Soul achieves this through its adopted instrument the human personality by virtue of its ability to express the qualities of the Soul—atma, buddhi and manas—whilst in physical incarnation.

Sutratma the life thread anchored in the heart and which links Monad Soul and physical body via the various permanent atoms (see also Monad and Permanent Atoms).

NOTES

INTRODUCTION
[1] Dr Douglas Baker, *The Jewel in the Lotus*, 2nd ed. (Essendon, Herts: Baker Publications, 1985), p15.

CHAPTER ONE
[1] The classical esoteric teachings state that there are five major initiations which occur during our long evolutionary sojourn prior to obtaining liberation from the Wheel of Rebirth. When the fifth initiation is reached we are then described as a Master or Adept. The five major initiations may be very briefly summarised as follows: The first initiation is when we experience the 'pull of the monad', the 'father in heaven' beckoning us towards the spiritual path. Many incarnations may take place before the second initiation when the Soul-orientated personality is able to discipline, control and transmute the various desires of the personality towards spiritual ends. The third initiation occurs when a fully integrated personality (being stable under all situations of involvement with the material world) is ready to serve as the instrument of the Soul which has learnt all of the necessary lessons upon the various rounds of the zodiac having successfully scaled the symbolic mountain of initiation. The personality has then been transfigured into a spiritual instrument and is now free to work in accordance with the divine plan. The fourth initiation occurs thereafter when all desires of the personality are renounced and spiritual service is our sole objective. These individuals are referred to as Arhats. At the fifth initiation our consciousness is transferred to the Fifth Kingdom of Souls. At this stage of our evolution every lesson relating to incarnation in physical form has been learned. The Wheel of Rebirth has served its purpose to unfold the flower of the Soul. A Master is free from the need to incarnate but may do so to assist in the process of evolution.
[2] Carl Jung, *Memories, Dreams, Reflections*, (New York: Vintage Books, 1989), 205.
[3] Joseph Campbell, *The Hero with a Thousand Faces*, (London: Fontana Press, 1993,) p30

CHAPTER TWO
[1] Dr Douglas Baker, *The Jewel in the Lotus*, p15.

CHAPTER THREE
[1] Brahman is a principle of the universe from the essence of which all emanates, and into which all returns. Beyond Brahman is Parabrahman, the Supreme Brahman and the self-enduring, eternal cause of all causes which encompasses Brahman.
[2] *Bhagavad Gita*, 10: 42.

[3] The word hylozoism is a compound one derived from the Greek language, hylo meaning 'wood' or the 'matter' out of which forms are created, and zoe denoting 'life'.

[4] H.P. Blavatsky, *The Key to Theosophy*, (London: Theosophical Publishing House Ltd, 1987,) pp183-4

CHAPTER FOUR

[1] *Fire*: the energy of the divine which is responsible for the entire process of creation and its subsequent return to source. There are three distinct fires here: 1) *Electric Fire*: is the propelling vital force of our universe and also its ceaseless destructive and formative power. This is the energy of pure spirit which blends with the fire of mind-Solar Fire and the fire of kundalini when spiritual initiation occurs. 2) *Solar Fire*: the fire of higher mind. 3) *Fire by Friction*: the fire inherent within matter and which sustains and nurtures the various physical forms found throughout our Solar system.

[2] Mahamanvantara is a Sanskrit term. Maha means 'great' and manvantara means 'period of manifestation'. The mahamanvantara of our solar system is the Life of Brahma referred to in the Hindu teachings which consists of 311 trillion and 40 billion terrestrial years.

[3] Dr Douglas Baker, *Meditation: The Theory and Practice*, 2nd ed. (Essendon, Herts: Baker Publications, 1987) p30

[4] The quadruplicities or modes of astrology divide the twelve zodiacal signs into three sets of four with each of these sharing a similar quality: Cardinal (Aries, Cancer, Libra and Capricorn); Fixed (Taurus, Leo, Scorpio and Aquarius) and Mutable (Gemini, Virgo, Sagittarius and Pisces). The location of the Sun, the Ascendant, or a preponderance of planets in the natal chart of an individual in a particular quadruplicity—Cardinal, Fixed or Mutable—does not necessarily indicate that the Soul is seeking expression upon the corresponding cross in its long evolutionary journey.

[5] The word yoga possesses a Sanskrit root yuj meaning 'to join; to unite; harness; or to come into union or conjunction with'.

CHAPTER FIVE

[1] Dr Douglas Baker, *The Jewel in the Lotus*, p58.

[2] The Ascendant or Rising Sign is located on the eastern horizon at the time of our birth. This is where the Soul imprints the personality at birth with a blueprint for its expression. The Rising Sign in the natal chart indicates one's deepest potential and the prime source of one's creative energy and wisdom. Through the Rising Sign, and related factors in the chart, the purpose of the Soul can be identified and the subject directed to suitable areas of life where this can be most suitably expressed.

CHAPTER SIX

[1] Annie Besant, *Ancient Wisdom*, (Adyar, India: Theosophical Publishing House, 1911), 211.

² The seven planes of consciousness are each comprised of seven sub-planes with these increasing in refinement in progression from the lowest to the highest. In the diagram at the beginning of the chapter the four lowest sub-planes of the Manasic plane are labelled as 'Mental' whilst the three highest are described as 'Manasic'.

CHAPTER SEVEN

¹ The Holy Bible, Galatians 6:7.

² Dr Douglas Baker, *The Jewel in the Lotus*, p58.

CHAPTER EIGHT

¹ Dr Douglas Baker, *Anthropogeny: The Esoteric History of Man's Origin*, (Essendon, Herts: Baker Publications, 1975) 41.

CHAPTER NINE

¹ This occurs through humanity's response to the archetypal energies that govern and direct the process of evolution, and to the morphic fields (as described by Rupert Sheldrake) which arise from such responses. This is discussed in Chapter 12.

² Paul Wright, *Why Quantum*, found at http://www.claregategroup.org/index.php/articles/why-quantum/

³ Sanat Kumara is the incarnation of the Planetary Logos. In the Christian Bible he is described as 'The Ancient of Days' and in Hindu scriptures as the 'First Kumara'.

CHAPTER TEN

¹ The Hindu Trimurti, as the three aspects of Brahman, describes the process of creation, maintenance and destruction within our universe thereby illustrating the effects of the three Major Rays.

² Ray Four of Art and Harmony Through Conflict is a combination of the energies of Ray One of Will and Power and Ray Two of Love-Wisdom; Ray Five of Concrete Knowledge and Science is a combination of the energies of Ray One and Ray Three of Active Intelligence; Ray Six of Idealism Devotion is a combination of the energies of Ray Two of and Ray Three; Ray Seven is a combination of the energies of Rays One, Two and Three.

³ There are three aspects to the Sun. The disc of the Sun is the body of manifestation of the Solar Logos in the same manner as the human body houses a human monad. The disc of the Sun radiates energies that sustain the physical forms of all lesser beings within the Solar Ring-Pass-Not. Behind the disc of the Sun there lies the Heart of the Sun from where the energies of the Seven Rays flow outwards to the planets within our solar system whereby their evolutionary energies urge all kingdoms and hierarchies of life towards their goal of Truth, Beauty and Goodness. The Central Spiritual Sun which lies within the Heart of the Sun is the spiritual hub where the Rays are received into our solar system. The disc of the Sun and the planets within our solar system represent the personality vehicles of the Solar Logos. The Heart of the Sun the Soul, and the Central Spiritual Sun the monad.

[4] Christianity, and therefore Catholicism, is powerfully influenced by the Sixth Ray of Idealism and Devotion. The Catholic Church also has a strong association with the Seventh Ray due to its application of ritual.

CHAPTER ELEVEN

[1] Dr Douglas Baker, *The Jewel in the Lotus*, p50.

[2] *Ibid.*, p51

[3] Heinrich Zimmer, *Myths and Symbols in Indian Art and Civilisation*, (Princeton, NJ :Princeton University Press, 1992) p137

[4] Joseph Campbell, *The Power of Myth*, with Bill Moyers from transcripts of the TV series. (New York: Anchor Books 1991) 210.

[5] *Ibid.*, p226

[6] Chandogya Upanishad 6. 8.7.

[7] Frieda Fordham, *An Introduction to Jung's Psychology*, (London: Penguin Books, 1953) p79.

CHAPTER TWELVE

[1] Carl Jung, *Man and his Symbols*, (London: Arkana, 1990) p83.

[2] *Ibid.*, p304

[3] The word archetype is a compound one derived from Greek language. Arkhe means 'first' or 'original' with typos meaning 'model' or 'type'. This offers us insight into their causal nature and origins.

[4] William Shakespeare, *As You Like It*, Act II Scene 7.

[5] In the use of the term 'elementary ideas' Campbell is referring to the concept of Elementargedanke, devised by the 19th century German polymath Adolf Bastian and which contributed to Jung's development of the theory of archetypes. Bastian argued for the 'psychic unity of mankind'.

[6] Joseph Campbell, *The Power of Myth*, p61.

[7] Carl Jung, *Man and his Symbols*, p67

CHAPTER THIRTEEN

[1] Roberto Assagioli, *Psychosynthesis: A Collection of Basic Writings*, (Amherst, Massachusetts, 2012) 14

[2] Despite certain similarities and an interrelationship between these, it is important to differentiate between the Jungian Shadow, being the dark and instinctual nature of our present incarnation, and the Dweller on the Threshold which consists of the sum total of our lower nature, including our fears, whose effects have been created over our many previous lives.

CHAPTER FOURTEEN

[1] Dr Douglas Baker, *Beyond the Intellect*, p156

[2] Joseph Campbell, *The Hero with a Thousand Faces*, p 259.

[3] *Ibid.*, p11.

CHAPTER FIFTEEN

[1] Carl Jung, *Man and his Symbols*, p39.

[2] The word symbol is a compound one derived from the Greek word symbolon. Sym means 'together' whilst bolon means 'thrown'. A symbol is thus 'that which has been thrown together'.

[3] Heinrich Zimmer, *Philosophies of India*, (New York: Princeton University Press, 1951) pp312-3.

[4] Carl Jung, *Man and his Symbols*, p50.

[5] *Ibid*.

[6] The Ouroboros is an ancient symbol depicting a dragon or serpent devouring its tail. This is held to symbolise infinity together with the cycle of life, death and rebirth leading to immortality as represented by the phoenix (see Chapter 20). It is also a symbol of primordial unity related to that existing in or persisting before any beginning and possessing such force or qualities that it cannot be extinguished. Jung viewed the Ouroboros as an archetype and the basic mandala of alchemy whereby it represented the individuation process and the unification of opposites.

[7] *Ibid*., pp20-1.

[8] *Ibid*., p53.

[9] Dr Douglas Baker, *The Psychology of Discipleship*, 2nd ed. (Essendon, Herts: Baker Publications 1991) p155.

[10] Chapter 22 describes how the human personality is partly constituted by what exponents of psychosynthesis refer to as 'sub-personalities'. These may be described as functions or aspects of an individual in whom various psychological qualities are not integrated into their overall personality structure. These are personality structures which we have developed as a means of coping with the circumstances that we have previously encountered, and particularly in our early years of life.

[11] *Ibid*., p66.

[12] Dr Douglas Baker, *In the Steps of the Master,* (Essendon, Herts: Baker Publications 1977) p157.

[13] Dr Douglas Baker, Beyond the Intellect, p43

CHAPTER SIXTEEN

[1] Dr Douglas Baker, *Beyond the Intellect*, (Essendon, Herts: Baker Publications 1979) p159.

[2] The stone refers to the 'philosopher's stone' which relates to the divine life force which, as we have seen, is both immanent and transcendent.

[3] A revered Islamic servant of God.

[4] Carl Jung, *Four Archetypes*, (New Jersey: Princeton University Press, 2012), p67.

CHAPTER SEVENTEEN

[1] Dr Douglas Baker, *Beyond the Intellect*, p90

[2] The conclusion of the Theseus myth occurs when he assumes the role of his father. The venturing hero had promised his father that if his mission were successful then he would display a white sail on his ship upon returning, rather than the usual black sail which would indicate that he had been killed. Theseus forgot to display the white sail and when his ship appeared on the horizon his

father Aegeus was overcome with grief and threw himself into the sea. Theseus then succeeded his father and was crowned King of Athens. The hero has demonstrated here the ability to overcome the challenges offered upon his quest whereby he may then adopt the role of the father—the monad or 'father in heaven'.

CHAPTER TWENTY

[1] As outlined in Chapter 12, the wisdom teachings diverge from current concepts of the collective unconscious in that they differentiate between their astral and mental effects and those energies which arise from the planes of Atma, Buddhi and Manas. The origin of the latter is therefore divine and reflects spiritual archetypes or 'divine ideas' rather than the instinctual, desire-driven expression of archetypal energies which are representative of the lower-mental, astral and etheric planes. When treading the path, one is seeking freedom from the conditioning and the constraints of the collective unconscious by accessing and expressing the energies of the 'superconscious'.

CHAPTER TWENTY ONE

[1] William Shakespeare, *As You Like It*, 1. Act II, Scene 1

[2] Roberto Assagioli. *Transpersonal Development: The Dimension Beyond Psychosynthesis*, (Findhorn, Forres: Smiling Wisdom an imprint of Inner Way Productions 2007), p76.

[3] Dr Douglas Baker, *The Jewel in the Lotus,* p181.

CHAPTER TWENTY TWO

[1] Roberto Assagioli. *Transpersonal Development: The Dimension Beyond Psychosynthesis*, p272.

[2] Roberto Assagioli T*he Act of Will: Guide to Self-Actualization and Self-Realization*, (Wellingborough, Northampton: Crucible an Imprint of the Aquarian Press, part of Thorsons Publishing Group 1990) p64.

[3] Dr Douglas Baker, *In the Steps of the Maste*r, p54

CHAPTER TWENTY THREE

[1] Alice Bailey, *Glamour: A World Problem*, (New York: Lucis Press, 1950) p39

[2] Dr Douglas Baker, *The Psychology of Discipleship*, p16.

BIBLIOGRAPHY

Assagioli. R. *Psychosynthesis: A Collection of Basic Writings*. Amherst, Massachusetts, 2012
—*The Act of Will: Guide to Self-Actualization and Self-Realization*, Wellingborough, Northampton: Crucible an Imprint of the Aquarian Press, part of Thorsons Publishing Group 1990
—*Transpersonal Development: The Dimension Beyond Psychosynthesis*, Findhorn, Forres: Smiling Wisdom an imprint of Inner Way Productions 2007

Bailey, A.A. *Discipleship in the New Age*. *Vol One*, New York: Lucis Press, 1944
—*Discipleship in the New Age*. *Vol Two*, New York: Lucis Press, 1955
—*Esoteric Astrology*, New York: Lucis Press, 1951
—*Esoteric Psychology. Vol 1*, New York: Lucis Press, 1936
—*Esoteric Psychology. Vol 2*. New York: Lucis Press, 1942
—*Glamour: A World Problem*, New York: Lucis Press, 1950
—*The Labours of Hercules*, London: Lucis Press, 1974

Baker, D. *Anthropogeny: The Esoteric History Of Man's Origin*. Essendon, Herts: Baker Publications, 1975
—*Beyond the Intellect*. Essendon, Herts: Baker Publications, 1979
—*Esoteric Astrology: A New Astrology for a New Millenium*. Essendon, Herts: Baker Publications 1998
—*Esoteric Psychology*. 3rd ed. Essendon, Herts: Baker Publications, 1996
—*In the Steps of the Master*. Essendon, Herts: Baker Publications, 1977
—*Superconsciousness Through Meditation*. 3rd ed. Essendon, Herts: Baker Publications, 1991
—*The Jewel in the Lotus*. 2nd ed. Essendon, Herts: Baker Publications, 1985
—*Meditation: The Theory and Practice*. 2nd ed. Essendon, Herts: Baker Publications, 1987
—*The Psychology of Discipleship*. Essendon, Herts: Baker Publications, 1991
—*The Spiritual Diary*. 2nd ed. Essendon, Herts: Baker Publications, 1980

Besant, A. *A Study in Consciousness*. London: Theosophical Publishing Society, 1915
—*The Ancient Wisdom*. Adyar, India: Theosophical Publishing House, 1911
Blavatsky. H.P. *The Key to Theosophy*. London: Theosophical Publishing House Ltd, 1987
—*The Secret Doctrine*. Adyar, India: Theosophical Publishing House, 1979

Campbell, J. *Goddesses: Mysteries of the Divine Feminine*. Novato, California: New World Library, 2013
—*Myths of Light: Eastern Metaphors of the Eternal*. Novato, California: New World Library, 2003
—*Pathways to Bliss: Mythology and Personal Transformation*. Novato, California: New World Library, 2004
—*The Hero with a Thousand Faces*. London: Fontana Press, 1993
—*The Power of Myth* with Bill Moyers from transcripts of the TV series. New York: Anchor Books 1991
—*Thou Art That: Transforming Religious Metaphor*. Novato, California: New World Library, 2001

Edinger, E. *Ego and Archetype*. Boston & London: Shambala, 1992
—*The Eternal Drama: The Inner Meaning of Greek Mythology*. Boston & London: Shambhala, 1994

Editors. *Hindu Scriptures*. London: Phoenix, 2005

Firman, J & Gila, A. *Psychosynthesis: A Psychology of the Spirit*. Albany, NY: State University of New York Press, 2002

Jung, C. *Four Archetypes*. New Jersey: Princeton University Press, 2012
—*Man and his Symbols*. London: Arkana, 1990
—*Memories, Dreams, Reflections*. New York: Vintage Books, 1989
—*Psychology and Alchemy*. London: Routledge, 2010

Fordham, F. *An Introduction to Jung's Psychology*. London: Penguin Books, 1953

Hodgkinson, B. *Essence of Vedanta*. Royston, Herts: Eagle Editions, 2006

Leadbeater, C.W. *Dreams; What They Are and How They Are Caused*. New York: Cosimo, 2007

Matthews, John ed., *At the Table of the Grail*. London: Watkins Publishing, 2002

Powell. A.E. *The Etheric Double*. London: Theosophical Publishing House, 1925
—*The Astral Body*. London: Theosophical Publishing House, 1926
—*The Mental Body*. London: Theosophical Publishing House, 1927
—*The Causal Body*. London: Theosophical Publishing House, 1928

Sheldrake, R. *The Presence of the Past*. London: Fontana, 1989

Zimmer, H. *Myths and Symbols in Indian Art and Civilisation*. Princeton, NJ: Princeton University Press, 1992
—*Philosophies of India*. New York: Princeton University Press, 1951

INDEX